D1257987

With love and light,

Kim T. H.

How Have You Loved?

Karen T. Hluchan

BALBOA.
PRESS

A DIVISION OF HAY HOUSE

Balboa Press books may be ordered through booksellers or by contacting:

Balboa Press
A Division of Hay House
1663 Liberty Drive
Bloomington, IN 47403
www.balboapress.com
1 (877) 407-4847

Because of the dynamic nature of the Internet, any web addresses or links contained in this book may have changed since publication and may no longer be valid. The views expressed in this work are solely those of the author and do not necessarily reflect the views of the publisher, and the publisher hereby disclaims any responsibility for them.

The author of this book does not dispense medical advice or prescribe the use of any technique as a form of treatment for physical, emotional, or medical problems without the advice of a physician, either directly or indirectly. The intent of the author is only to offer information of a general nature to help you in your quest for emotional and spiritual well-being. In the event you use any of the information in this book for yourself, which is your constitutional right, the author and the publisher assume no responsibility for your actions.

Any people depicted in stock imagery provided by Thinkstock are models, and such images are being used for illustrative purposes only. Certain stock imagery © Thinkstock.

Printed in the United States of America.

ISBN: 978-1-4525-8714-1 (sc)
ISBN: 978-1-4525-8715-8 (hc)
ISBN: 978-1-4525-8713-4 (e)

Library of Congress Control Number: 2013920736

Balboa Press rev. date: 4/17/2014

With light and love
to the beautiful spirits of all beings

Contents

Foreword xi

Introduction xiii

    How Have You Loved? xiii

Thoughts Are Powerful Energy 1

    Our Thoughts Determine Our Destinies 3

    Reacting Positively to Negative Circumstances 8

    How Stressful Thoughts and Emotions Can Affect Us Physically 13

    Live in the Present by Letting Go of Fear, Regret, and Worry 20

    Forgiving Means Moving Forward 23

    Happiness Is a Choice 26

    Gratitude: Appreciating What You Have 30

Embrace the Love within Your Heart 37

    Falling in Love with Your True Self 39

    Be True to Yourself 46

    Balancing Giving and Receiving 50

    Knowing You Are Not Alone on Your Journey through Life 59

    Reaching Out to Your Heavenly Support Team 64

    Handling Situations That Test Your Faith 67

    Living with Absolute Faith in Your Dreams 75

The Gifts of Mediumship 81

    What Happens When We Cross Over into Heaven? 83

    Coping with the Loss of a Loved One 91

    Pets and Animals Go to Heaven, Too!.................................... 99

    How You Can Prepare for a Spirit Reading with a Medium........... 102

    How Spirit Communicates with Mediums............................. 114

    Receiving Messages from Spirit through Our Senses...................... 125

    Utilizing Your Intuition.. 139

    Meditation Connects You to the Source and Your Soul................. 143

    Deciphering the Messages within Your Dreams 148

    The Beauty and Messages in Music.. 156

Sharing the Love..161

    There Are Two Motivating Factors: Love and Fear...................... 163

    Reasons for Being...171

    Unity, Peace, and Love..176

    How We Can Be Angels on Earth...................................... 179

    Bringing Out the Best in Yourself and Others........................ 182

The Wonders of Nature.. 187

    Our Spiritual Relationship with Animals 189

    Signs Sent by Heaven through the Animal Kingdom...................... 193

    Meditating with Nature 199

    The Power of the Ocean..202

    Crystals: Treasures of the Earth 207

    Reiki Energy Healing..214

We Are One...219

    Connected by Love...221

Afterword..225

Acknowledgments 227

Bibliography...231

Index 233

Foreword

Karen came into our lives after a very tragic event. We had lost an unborn child, and we were having a hard time moving on with our lives because of the tremendous amount of grief, negative thoughts, and personal blame that we were carrying within our hearts.

Karen is the type of person that, when you meet her, you feel as if you have known her your entire life. She is filled with love and brings peace to your heart, mind, and spirit. The first time we met her, we were getting together with her for a spirit medium reading that impacted our lives in ways we never imagined. As a result of the reading Karen provided, we were able to release the negativity that was preventing us from moving forward. She was able to put everything into perspective in order for us to begin healing from within. Furthermore, Karen helped us to realize how unfortunate events often serve a higher purpose for the growth of our souls. Once we understood how we were allowing negative events to rule our lives, we were able to turn our lives around and clear our paths for happiness, which included the blessing of a healthy pregnancy in the weeks following our reading with her.

After our personal experiences with Karen, we were excited to read *How Have You Loved?* Her clear and easy-to-understand guidance throughout the book taught us how to work on creating a positive outlook through our thoughts, how to love ourselves and others, how mediumship works and what happens to our souls when we cross over, and how nature and spirit play important roles in our lives. Most importantly, we recognized that by ignoring our inner voices, we were not utilizing the help God and the angels were trying to give us. Karen taught us how to listen to the messages we receive from our intuition, because they are direct communications from spirit trying to lead us in the right direction. Once we began to truly pay attention and listen to our intuition and our hearts, we were rewarded with a much happier life.

We are ecstatic to know you now have the opportunity to experience Karen's words of wisdom firsthand. She breaks down the mystery of what happens to our souls when we cross over and reassures us that we are reunited with our loved ones who have passed before us. Knowing they help us with our lives, as well as with our transitions into heaven, has given us great comfort. We truly feel that meeting Karen and reading this book have definitively changed our lives for the better. We are confident that you will have the same experience once you have read the healing guidance Karen provides in *How Have You Loved?*

With peaceful hearts and love,
Jennifer and Frank Petronis

Introduction

How Have You Loved?

The Most Important Question You Will Answer

When our physical bodies expire and our spirits make the journey to heaven, many extraordinary events take place. One of those events is the nonjudgmental review of our lives from the viewpoint of heaven. As we delve into the decisions we made and the actions we took, there is one very important question we need to answer that sums up our entire existence as spiritual beings on a human journey. The question is: How have you loved?

The answer to this question is determined by how you loved yourself and others, as well as how receptive you were to the love that was given to you. Think about it. If that is the most important question you will answer when you review your life in heaven, how will that change how you live your life today? Do you freely give and receive love on a daily basis?

Upon receiving this revelation from heaven, I was greatly inspired to share the insights about our divine life purposes that I have acquired through deep contemplation, active observation of human behavior, and blessed communication with spiritual beings.

How Have You Loved? is a journey about exploring how your thoughts determine your destiny, discovering the love within your heart, understanding the gifts of mediumship and our connection in spirit with one another, sharing the love within your heart, and appreciating the role nature plays in the development of your soul plan.

What began as a series of short articles that I wrote and published on a weekly basis has evolved and developed into an expanded collection of guidance inspired by heaven. Each section and chapter is designed to bring to light the solutions, ideas, and concepts that enable you to live your life to the fullest and with the most joy. I hope you enjoy your adventure through *How Have You Loved?* as much as I have loved writing it and living it.

On a personal note, throughout *How Have You Loved?* I refer to our Creator as *God* with masculine pronouns, such as *he* or *him*. Due to my cultural upbringing, that is the terminology I am most comfortable using when referring to the Supreme Being that created our beautiful spirits. It is important to note that our Creator is non-denominational and non-gender specific. You may feel more comfortable mentally inserting your own cultural terminology and references, as our Creator is referred to by many names and is, in essence, the same Supreme Being that watches over us all.

From my spirit to yours, I present this gift from heaven to you with everlasting love from your heavenly support team. May your light shine more brightly in the world because of it.

Namaste!

Thoughts
Are
Powerful Energy

♥

Our Thoughts Determine Our Destinies

The thoughts that swirl in our minds are extremely powerful. They set the stage for our outlooks, how we react to the situations we encounter, what we dream of and hope for, and—most importantly—they determine our destinies. It is important to know that thoughts are a form of powerful energy that defines what we attract to ourselves and guides the paths our lives take. Our thoughts truly do determine our destinies and by knowing this, you can learn how to best utilize them, as well as control the negative thoughts that attempt to derail you from your life purpose.

It may seem as though we have no control over the thoughts that pop into our heads, but we do. We can train our brains to shut out the negative thought patterns and bring forth the positive, enriching thoughts that help guide us to opportunities for growth and the manifestation of our dreams.

The Purpose of the Ego and Negative Thoughts

Negative thoughts that enter our minds are challenges to the positive experiences of life that we truly deserve. They are the thoughts that say we could not possibly succeed or we are unattractive or failures. This is the voice of the ego. The negative thoughts that come from the ego can intrude and create a mind-set that is counterproductive to our personal happiness. When we are in heaven, these thoughts do not permeate our spirits; however, here on earth, where we are on the fast track to learning life lessons for the purpose of evolving our souls, negative situations and thoughts are obstacles that we are meant to overcome. They can help us to be the best we can be. It all depends upon the actions we do or do not take to surmount their presence, persistence, and effects.

Welcoming Positive Thinking

Have you ever heard about the power that comes from positive thinking? Have you ever truly tried to live it? As you begin your journey of incorporating more positive thinking into your outlook, start by becoming more aware of the negative thoughts that enter your mind. Dismiss them as soon as you recognize their presence, and counter them with positive thoughts. If the negative thoughts persist, stop what you are doing. Look around and find something you are grateful for in that exact moment. For instance, you could be appreciative of the way the sun is filtering through the trees, the relationship you have with your best friend, or even the clothes on your back. It can be anything that makes you happy. The point of this exercise is to replace the negative thoughts with positive ones. Once you have identified something you are grateful for, take the exercise one step further by performing an activity that makes you happy, such as reading a book, taking a walk, or working on a hobby. This positive distraction will move your mind away from the negative soundtrack that was taking over your thoughts. Keep in mind that it takes practice to reprogram your mind. It is the same as breaking yourself of a bad habit. The more you work at it, the easier it becomes and the quicker you will recognize when pessimism is attempting to encroach upon your life.

Manifesting Dreams with Positive Thinking

There are some wonderful dreams I would like to see manifested in my life. Likewise, I am sure there are dreams you would like to see manifested in your life. To begin my journey, I make a conscious decision to actively send out positive thoughts toward my true heart's desires. Then, I ask God and the angels to help me to achieve them. I let go of trying to make these dreams manifest on my own because I know my vision here on earth is limited. I also know that trying to force a situation to come to fruition can actually prevent it from happening. God and the angels see more than we do and can help guide us on the right path. I know I must open myself up to the guidance they give me and strive to keep my thoughts about my dreams positive. I do this by visualizing a bright light around my dreams and imagining my desired outcomes as already realized. In my heart, I rest easy knowing that God and the angels have received and acknowledged my visions, and are actively in the process of manifesting my true goals and desires.

For your dreams, open your mind and imagination. Visualize your deepest desires and dreams coming true. See yourself basking in the happiness that is truly yours to live. Your dreams are meant to come true, regardless of the circumstances that surround you. If we can dream it, we can live it. All we have to do is truly believe with all of our hearts that we not only deserve this happiness, but also can experience the actualization of our dreams in our lifetimes here on earth, not just in heaven.

Stay the Course

Keep in mind that the way in which our dreams manifest may involve circumstances that appear negative on the surface. Let go of the momentary disappointment caused by the twists and turns our lives take, as these seemingly negative circumstances or events may be necessary in order to clear out obstacles that were impeding our progress. Be open to change, take it all in stride, and take time each day to acknowledge with gratitude the positive events and circumstances in your life. Keep visualizing your actualized dream. The angels, who assist God with the manifestation of your happiness, will help you. All you have to do is ask them for their help, give them permission to intervene on your behalf, and truly believe that they are assisting you.

Heavenly Help

As we grow from infants to adults, various circumstances and people influence and shape the way we perceive the world. It is during this time that we learn about happiness, sadness, confidence, fear, assurance, worry, contentedness, and regret. The negativity we are exposed to can become a way of life, or we can choose to disregard the negative and hurtful programming by following our own hearts and paths toward happiness. It takes a strong belief in yourself and strength of will in order to shift negative thought patterns into positive, life-affirming ways of thinking. The good news is that we do not have to make this journey alone. We have each other, as well as our *heavenly support teams* of God, the angels, spirit guides, past spiritual masters, and deceased loved ones, to assist us.

Dream your dreams and diligently work on keeping your thoughts positive. I know it can be challenging at times, because I face the same obstacles as you. When I encounter challenges, I call upon my heavenly support team to help me elevate my thoughts, and I express my gratitude to them for lending me their loving strength. Your heavenly support team is there to assist you, too, with your dreams, your thoughts, and your love. Ask your team for guidance and support, release your worries, and trust that they are working diligently on your behalf. Maintain an open mind about the way in which your requests will be answered. Keep in mind that patience is needed, as it takes time and resources to orchestrate the intricate pathways to your desired outcomes.

♥

Reacting Positively
to Negative Circumstances

We are all here on this earth at this particular time to assist one another as we work toward the evolvement of our souls. Unfortunately, not everyone understands this concept. Negative events and painful circumstances, as well as familial and cultural influences, could be the reason why some people resort to behaviors that are hurtful toward others, including selfishness. This does not mean that all hope is lost for them; it may mean that they have not yet been exposed to information or experiences that could help them to understand the benefits of working together. You can attempt to help this person to see how his or her behavior is harmful; however, it is not necessary to expend energy on someone who refuses to listen or learn. Share and help where you can, but know that it is ultimately up to each individual to make the choices that are most appropriate for his or her own life.

It is important to note that we are all on different levels with our soul evolvement. In light of that, we should do our best not to look down on people who have not yet learned to overcome the fear of getting hurt by others. Often, it is a lack of trust that drives someone to focus only upon themselves. We are all here to learn, and even though someone may appear to be on a different level than you, it does not mean he or she is better or worse off. Instead, it may indicate that the person is concentrating on different lessons or is operating under a soul contract that helps him or her to evolve and learn through the incorporation of negative circumstances. Either way, we all experience major events within our lives that are designed for the growth of our souls and the successful completion of life lessons. By supporting one another, we are contributing positive energy in the form of loving kindness to each other, as well as to the world.

Conscious Choices and Honest Assessments

Throughout our lives, we will encounter many situations that test our abilities to maintain a positive state of mind. Turmoil erupts when fear is the primary emotion motivating someone's actions. This is because it drives people to take action based on negative emotions, such as jealousy, anger, greed, or selfishness.

When you are caught up in a scenario in which someone is causing you pain through his or her actions, it is sometimes difficult to prevent an automatic reaction that mirrors or feeds into another person's detrimental behaviors. It can be very challenging at times to counter negativity with positive actions because our own shock and pain need to be dealt with before we can proceed. Sometimes, our first instincts are to lash out at the person or people who hurt us.

If anger or pain is coloring your thoughts, take a few steps back from the source of the negativity. Look at the situation from all points of view through an honest assessment of the behaviors of everyone involved. Once you have had a chance to calm your thoughts and truthfully evaluate the situation, your mind will be free to come up with ideas or solutions that have the potential to create the most positive outcome for everyone.

You can break the chain of negativity by looking for the underlying reasons behind the person's behavior and counter it with understanding and kindness without undermining your values or self-esteem. For instance, a friend of yours lashes out at you for going out to lunch with another friend. Jealousy and a feeling of inadequacy may be the emotions that are triggering her behavior. Her feelings are her responsibility and not yours, and they may be rooted in past relationships in which she has been betrayed. Calmly let your friend know that while you appreciate her friendship, you do have other people in your life you like to spend time with as well. Let your friend know that you care about her and that your actions were in no way a threat to your relationship with her. If she continues to conduct herself in a manner that is harmful or hurtful to you, you can choose to walk away and not allow the negativity to infiltrate your life. In situations such as this, it is important to listen to your heart. You do not have to stay in a relationship that is not healthy. If you need help in dealing with the issues you face, ask God and the angels for support and guidance regarding the best path for you to take. They will provide answers to you through your intuition, as well as through external signs and messages, which will point you in the direction that is right for you.

Resolving Differences

While attempting to resolve differences, it is imperative to be honest with yourself and others. Do your best to let go of any anger that has built up inside of you, as it is unproductive and blocks open communication. Confronting people while angry almost guarantees that they will not hear you because their defenses will be up. Instead, set up a time to talk about the situation with the person or people involved when you are calm. In this manner, you will have a better chance of resolving the issue in the most positive way for all concerned. Present your ideas, actively listen to the feedback you receive, work through the issue by allowing each person to express his or her thoughts, and do your best to move past the problem. Many times, it is a misunderstanding or communication breakdown that is the cause of the problem. We are all human, and we all make mistakes. In order to move past the errors we make and to repair our relationships, we need to be able to listen, speak, and respond in a manner that shows respect to all, including ourselves. Remember to extend forgiveness and to release the issue. Apologize sincerely if it was your actions that caused the rift or made the situation worse. Wallowing in the past and dredging it up again and again only hurts you in the end, because you are repeatedly impaling yourself with old pain regarding a situation that is beyond altering. Let it go and live in the present.

Healthy Closure

If in your contemplation or discussions you realize that the best solution would be to end the relationship due to irreconcilable differences, bring it to a close with kindness, grace, and honor. Wish the person well, pray for his or her health and happiness, and move on with your life. Often, the ending is a blessing in disguise because it may clear the way for an even better relationship or set of circumstances that could not have happened until you released this particular relationship from your life.

Taking Responsibility for Your Own Actions

When you behave in a manner that causes pain to others, apologize to the person or people you hurt. It does happen. We all have moments when we wish we would have reacted in a different way. No one is perfect. The key is to recognize your mistakes and make amends as soon as you are able. Let the parties involved know you are sorry, and mean it by not repeating the same negative or hurtful behavior. This will go a long way toward mending your relationships. Forgive yourself, too. We all make mistakes; it is a part of life and the experience gives us an opportunity to learn how to be better people. By recognizing and taking responsibility for our actions, we are actively taking part in the evolvement of our own souls while mindfully respecting the spirit of others.

Strive to be the best person you can be despite any turmoil that may be around you. Remember, you are actively in the process of learning, too. We all stumble from time to time, but if we strive to take the high road and choose to counter negative situations with positive reactions, both our lives and the lives of those around us will be happier. We cannot control all of the events that occur in our lives, nor can we control the behaviors of others. We can control our own actions and reactions, though, and decide to look beyond the negative behaviors of others by displaying understanding, kindness, and grace in the face of adversity and turmoil. By doing so, you will be welcoming peace and calm into your own life. At the same time, you will be showing others that fears and chaos are often based on misunderstandings that can be resolved, or even prevented, with compassion and empathy. In this way, we fulfill our soul contracts to help each other as we live our lives on this earth and evolve as souls.

How Stressful Thoughts and Emotions Can Affect Us Physically

Upsetting situations, as well as negative thoughts and emotions, can physically manifest in a variety of ways, such as panic attacks, tendonitis, headaches, and mysterious aches and pains. My personal experience includes emotional overeating that I felt helpless to stop. Food is necessary for sustenance, and it is one substance we cannot avoid if we are to continue to live. It can be very challenging to overcome problems with the over-consumption or under-consumption of food for that very reason. Moreover, the social aspect of eating meals together and at celebrations can greatly contribute to the anxiety of someone who is having difficulty maintaining a healthy relationship with the food he or she consumes. It is hard, sometimes, for people to recognize the reason for over-eating or under-eating because it requires them to look deep within themselves to see the reasons why they are using food as a substitute for happiness or controlling food intake to the point of malnutrition. Instead of feeling shame when we are experiencing a problem and trying to hide it, we can help ourselves by extending kindness, love, understanding, and forgiveness toward our own soul when a problem exists. The pain behind these issues is real, and the sooner we recognize the actual reasons behind it, the quicker we can begin the healing process.

Consuming Stress

Emotional over-eating is a sign that we are internalizing our stress—we are eating as a way of triggering happy hormones that are not being triggered by our life experiences. This is the same reason some people turn to drugs or alcohol—to temporarily ease deeply rooted unhappiness or problems. As an example, I know when I start eating chocolate and enriched white-flour products on a daily basis, I need to take a look at what is causing me to feel anxious or stressed. Usually, there is an underlying reason for eating the less healthful foods that has nothing to do with budget or time for cooking. For me, it has been unhappiness with relationships or job situations that I knew in my heart were not the right fit for me. I kept trying to make these situations work, and when my efforts did not produce the results I was looking for, praying for, and hoping for, I fell back into eating sugar and empty carbs as a way of bringing myself temporary relief from the emotional pain I was experiencing.

Ever Vigilant

Today, heavy consumption of sugary products is a wake-up call for me that a positive change needs to occur in my life. In other words, my higher self is giving me a blinking neon sign that I am in emotional pain. The same goes for people who reduce their eating to next to nothing, binge eat, or are obsessed with maintaining extremely rigid diets. Both over-eating and under-eating are strong messages from your soul indicating that you may be experiencing emotional pain due to external circumstances. It could be that you are carrying around guilt, you have not yet learned to appreciate yourself for who you are, or you feel powerless to change a stressful situation. There are many reasons as to why you may be experiencing emotional pain. Recognizing the reason and knowing you have the power within you to change your reactionary behavior is crucial to the successful healing of your spirit.

Unsatisfying Replacements for Our Souls

Over-eating is a way of satisfying our desire to feel happy, even if it is only for a moment or two when we taste our favorite comfort foods, which trigger the release of the happy endorphins in our brains. On the other side of the spectrum, starving ourselves or maintaining an extremely rigid diet is a sign of trying to gain control. Significant life-altering circumstances, such as the death of a loved one, the loss of a job, or a divorce, can make us feel as though our lives are out of our hands. One part of our lives that we can control is what we consume and how much we exercise. That is when obsession with control has the opportunity to take over, commencing the battle between your body's nutritional needs and your need to control a specific aspect in your life that relies solely on your efforts.

When you are eating too much or too little on a consistent basis, it could be a response to feelings about yourself or situations you may not want to face. As you open up and begin to recognize the underlying causes of eating disorders, it is good to know that you are not alone. Ask for help from the people around you, seek out professional help if it is needed, and ask God and your angels to help you to process the emotional pain that is behind your actions. Most of all, be patient and understanding with yourself by taking each day of your healing and recovery one step at a time. There may be times when you take a few steps backward into old habits. When that happens, recognize it as a lapse and get yourself back on track with the healing process. Know that you can overcome any obstacles that cross your path.

Wake-Up Call

I recently had another wake-up call myself. I knew I was over-eating due to a difficult employment situation; however, I found it challenging to stop myself from eating the junky foods that made me feel sluggish and unmotivated. On top of that, I was experiencing difficulties in a romantic relationship. I prayed to the angels to help me to improve my work situation and my relationship, as well as my eating habits. In time, the angels answered my prayers. This was not an occurrence that happened overnight, nor did it come without deep soul-searching for positive solutions. Once I asked for help, I knew I had to have patience and trust that God and the angels were working on my situations. It was my trust and faith that brought me inner peace while I continued to deal with highly stressful conditions in my job and my love life. With timing that was truly perfect, God and the angels intervened by dramatically changing my job situation through what may have appeared to be negative circumstances. In actuality, those circumstances cleared the way for me to follow my dreams as a medium. The angels also helped me to end the romantic relationship that brought me more pain than happiness. They orchestrated events in a way that made it close to impossible for me not to see that the best route was to release the unhealthy situations. Instead of feeling pain, I felt the release of the burdens I was carrying. Once I was free, I could see how I had allowed the situations to go on as long as they did. For too long, I put the welfare of others before my own. The angels showed me that it was time to take care of myself and to believe that I deserve to be in supportive, loving environments that include a healthy balance of giving and receiving.

Self-love and a firm belief in the care and love I receive from God and the angels gave me the serenity I needed to heal and move forward with my life. My prayers were answered in a way that was even better than I had imagined. This would not have happened if I had not placed my full trust and faith in God and the angels, because my disbelief would have blocked me from hearing their guidance and I would have gotten in my own way, as well as theirs. It is important to learn when to surrender control over to God and when it is time to take action. Having patience can be hard; however, by knowing that heaven will answer your prayers at the perfect time, you can accept the circumstances you are in as a necessary part of your path.

At times, there are lessons to be learned prior to your prayers being answered, which may include the realization that you are worthy of love and abundance. If there is a delay, make the most of it by enjoying activities that you can do on your own or with good friends. Remain open to opportunities that may very well be the answers to your prayers. Even if you do not understand how events fit in with the overall concept you have for your dreams, know that there may be a hidden dynamic that will be revealed when you are ready to recognize the gifts that you have been given.

Getting Past the Problems

Once I was removed from the stressful situations, I was no longer craving or eating empty carbs and chocolate every day. I still have to work on dropping the extra pounds I gained; however, I know that, in time, I will lose them through exercise I enjoy and getting back to making and eating healthy meals. By recognizing the problems that led to my poor eating habits, I can work on improving the underlying issues, as well as preventing the unnecessary ingestion of excess food as a substitute for happiness. I will need to remain vigilant, though, as it is easy to slip back into old habits. Throughout this transition, I discovered a deep love and appreciation for myself, as well as for all people who struggle with eating disorders.

The Power to Change Is within Us

When I was immersed in the stressful situations, I did not realize that I was literally consuming my stress in the form of food. Once I was no longer suffering, it became exceedingly clear that my harmful eating habits were due to the great unhappiness I felt powerless to change. It is important to note that even though I felt powerless, I was not. Instead of dealing with my feelings of unhappiness, I chose to attempt to escape them by temporarily blotting them out with unhealthy foods.

Have Faith

Once you have asked for help, have faith that your heavenly support team will guide you into situations that will enable you to release yourself from unhealthy habits. Your team's support may involve guiding you toward a professional who specializes in eating disorders or nutrition, removing you from harmful situations while at the same time providing enlightenment about the harm you were doing to yourself, or guiding you to a source where you can find a counselor who works within the light and can help to you to recognize the problems at hand.

Spirit Is with You

As you work through the underlying issues that led to an eating disorder, know that spiritual beings support you. You are not alone. God and the angels are there for you every step of the way. They are never too busy for you, as they can be in many places at once. Embrace their help as they envelop you with their light and help you to make your own light shine brighter.

Live in the Present by Letting Go of Fear, Regret, and Worry

Another way of diminishing the effects of negative thoughts and bringing in the positive is to live in the present. It can become a way of life that allows you to enjoy each moment as it comes. By focusing on what is right in front of us now, we open ourselves up to the opportunities that are present in this moment. People often wonder why, when we get older, time seems to disappear in a flash. We turn around, and weeks, months, or even years have passed. I used to think it was the increase in responsibilities as we got older that made time fly. As children, we have no concerns except for living in the moment. An epiphany sent by heaven helped me to realize that it is the concept of living in the moment, and not the responsibilities themselves, which enables us to live our lives to the fullest potential. It is our worries, regrets, and fears that rob us of our time, opportunities, and experiences because they drive our awareness away from the present—the only time in which we can make changes and savor the moments as they occur in our lives.

By worrying about what could be, we are not living in the present or paying attention to our immediate surroundings because we are too busy creating scenarios in our heads. With regrets, it is a replaying of past experiences and situations in our heads that blocks our vision. Worries and regrets are the children of fear, and fear is what prevents us from taking positive action in our lives.

Be Here Now

To clear your mind and live in the present, start by making yourself more aware of your patterns of thinking. When you catch yourself getting wrapped up in worries, regrets, or fears, stop the negative mind chatter by telling it to take a backseat and remind yourself to be here now, because right now is what living is all about.

This does not mean that you never look forward or back. From time to time, we all need to look forward to make plans and back to learn lessons from the past. Make plans for the future and look back to see what you could have done better, and then release it from your mind. Know that God and the angels have heard your thoughts and prayers. They will help you to answer them if you give them the chance to step in and set up the circumstances that will bring your dreams to fruition. There is no need to obsess about either the past or the future, as your destiny is being guided and cared for by extraordinary beings who have your best welfare at heart.

Count Your Blessings

To bring yourself back to the present, open your eyes and look around. Using the same practices we used to introduce positive thinking into your repertoire, find something you are grateful for in your life at this very moment—whether it is for the warmth of the sun, a friend sitting beside you, the blessing of good health, or the roof over your head. It does not matter what you select, only that you choose something that is right in front of you now. Savor all blessings, large and small, and recognize the joy of the moment within yourself. You can recognize this moment within your own thoughts, share it out loud, or write it down as a reminder of the beauty you can experience in each moment of your life.

Cherish Each Moment

There are wonderful people, signs, and opportunities right in front of you. By keeping your eyes open and your mind on the present, you give yourself the opportunity to make the most of your time and, more importantly, you give God and the angels the chance to step in and help guide you in decisions that lead to your greatest happiness. They place opportunities and signs in front of you all of the time. All you need to do is open your eyes to the wonders of the present to be the beneficiary of these great gifts. You may even find, like I did, that time seems to slow down. When you savor each moment for what it is, you are not only living your life to the fullest, but also as it is meant to be.

Forgiving Means Moving Forward

By extending forgiveness toward the people who have caused you pain, including yourself, you are releasing the negative energies you have accumulated and held within you from past experiences. This spring cleaning of emotional baggage cleanses the energy of your spirit, making it lighter and more buoyant, and frees up space in your life for positive thoughts, energy, and experiences. It is important to point out that forgiving people for past behaviors does not, by any means, imply that you condone their behaviors; rather, it releases you from a repetitive cycle of negative thinking that can be detrimental to your growth and evolvement as a soul.

The Heavy, Black Cloak

When we hold a grudge against someone, we are the one carrying around the negativity, not the person who hurt us. It is like wearing a heavy, black cloak that trips us up, weighs us down, and traps us in its gloom. Its darkness keeps us wrapped in a victim mentality that can draw even more negativity toward us. Additionally, the person or persons against whom you hold a grudge are not consciously affected by the negativity that cloaks your thoughts. In many cases, they are living their own lives, not even aware of the anger or upset you are carrying within you every day. The energy and time you are using to carry that grudge can be used instead to improve the quality of your life and move you forward toward your dreams. Moreover, by forgiving someone, you are acknowledging that they, like you, make mistakes—sometimes big mistakes, sometimes small mistakes. Forgiveness is one of the ways we can learn how to become the best that we can be, as mistakes allow us to see what does not work. The next step is to discard the methodology that caused you to make the mistake in the first place and start working toward a better solution.

Understanding through Compassion

Forgiveness means recognizing that the person or persons who committed injustices toward you were misguided. Somewhere along the line, they received faulty or inadequate information about how to behave with compassion toward another soul. As souls traveling onward on our own unique journeys, we need to recognize that not everyone is on the same level of evolvement. It does not mean that one soul is better than another; it just means that we all have lessons to learn in life and the person who hurt you has yet to learn the particular lesson that led him or her to bring you pain. Keep in mind that you, too, have lessons yet to learn and you may make mistakes along the way that could cause someone else distress. When you recognize your own mistakes, it is important to learn from those mistakes and extend forgiveness toward yourself. If possible, apologize to the person or people you have hurt and do your best not to repeat the same mistake in the future.

Releasing the Pain

To truly forgive another or yourself, acknowledge the pain and let it go. Know that everyone, including you, makes mistakes. You cannot control the actions of others; however, you can control yourself and how you react or respond to the events that occur in your life. Part of that control is in learning how to release negative feelings about the errors you have made and to move forward on a more positive path.

When forgiving others, you do not have to see the person face-to-face, nor do you need to re-enter a harmful relationship or put yourself in a negative situation in order to extend forgiveness. You can say it out loud to the universe or in your own mind. Surround the situation with God's loving light and visualize it as healed for both yourself and the other person or people involved. Whenever you find the heavy, black cloak of negativity trying to slip itself back upon your shoulders, remind yourself that you have already forgiven the past and let it go. If you feel you need help forgiving others, ask God and the angels to lend you their strength and support as you take these positive steps in your life. Your heavenly support team is always there for you if you need them—all you have to do is ask.

Happiness Is a Choice

Ultimately, you are responsible for your own happiness. This is because you are in full control of how you react to situations and people. The only being you are in control of is you. You cannot compel someone to behave in a certain way because we all have free will. The choices we make are entirely ours. When a seemingly negative event occurs, you can choose to let the negativity take over your psyche or you can opt to look for the positive in the situation and learn what you can from it. There are always healthy, positive lessons that can be learned from experiences that appear negative on the surface. The key to happiness is in choosing to look past the immediate negativity of circumstances in order to see the blessing that is intended for your soul's progression.

People Who Perpetually Complain

There are people I have encountered that never seem to be happy, even when what they have asked for is delivered to them. When their dreams and answers to their prayers are presented to them, they pick them apart, overlooking the positive and diving deep to find something to complain about. Most of the time, it is some small, nitpicky detail that most people would not think twice about; however, they choose to blow it out of proportion and let it ruin their experience. These people *choose* to live their lives in misery and often blame other people and circumstances for their problems. What they are not seeing is that they are the ones who are responsible for their actions and reactions. It is true that other people may cause a negative situation to appear in your life; however, you do not have to let it take you down a path of destruction and self-pity. You can choose to recognize the situation for what it is, determine the path you are going to take to improve the situation, learn from it, and move on. Our reactions determine our personal level of happiness. It is entirely up to us whether we mire ourselves in negativity or choose a more positive path.

Walking Away Is an Option

Recently, I spent some time in the company of a person who turned out to be a habitual complainer. Nothing could please this person. A small group of us were enjoying a holiday at a beautiful destination where the sun was shining and people were genuinely happy and smiling. This person, though, spent her days moping and grumbling. What is amazing, though, is that this person had been looking forward to taking this trip for a very long time, and when she finally got there, all she did was complain and state that she could not wait to leave. I have come across many people like this in my life and I have learned how to prevent their sour moods from ruining my vacations or my day. When I encounter such behavior, I may attempt, at first, to try to get them to see the wonder and beauty around them. If they cannot see it and continue to complain, I simply walk away and decide to enjoy my day by choosing to remove myself from a situation that has the potential to drag me down. I like to think of it as preventative maintenance for my soul.

Energy Is Contagious

Both positivity and negativity are contagious. Since I prefer to remain in a positive state of mind, I counter people's negative behavior toward me or words of complaint with positive observations. The people that respond best to this tactic are the ones that display only infrequent moodiness. For those who choose to remain in a state of perpetual complaining, any efforts to uplift their moods are often met with stronger disdain and, of course, more grumbling. The person who displays this type of behavior typically takes no responsibility for his or her state of mind and blames other people, as well as external factors, for his or her distress.

What people who display this behavior do not realize is that they are the only ones responsible for their foul moods. They actively choose to be miserable, just as I choose to maintain a state of mind that is clear, open, and receptive to optimistic energy and outcomes. Do not get me wrong, I do experience upsets in my life; however, I have learned to recognize that unfortunate events sometimes occur in order to clear the way for something better to enter my life. The time I spend being upset gets shorter and shorter as I realize that not everything is as it seems on the surface. When I choose to remain calm and optimistic in the face of adversity by trusting in God and the angels, I have found that the outcomes of my situations exceed my expectations and directly answer my most heartfelt prayers and dreams. All of this is available to you, too. Again, the choice is yours regarding whether or not you would like to invite the guidance and infinite wisdom of heaven to assist you with your life.

Making a Conscious Choice

By choosing to be happy, you are not only opening yourself up to wonderful opportunities and experiences, but also showing your heavenly support team your appreciation and gratitude for the gifts they bestow upon you every day. Complaining about a gift is a great way to ensure you will not get another and it will also alienate you from the givers and the people around you—which, by the way, may give you more fodder for complaining. As an alternative, you can choose to move beyond the negativity and open yourself up to the life you were meant to live with happiness and joy. God and the angels want us all to live happy, fulfilling lives and will assist us as long as we give them permission to do so. The choice is completely up to us regarding whether or not we choose to accept the gifts they so graciously give in the spirit of love.

Gratitude: Appreciating What You Have

Another way of maintaining a positive outlook is to express gratitude for what you do have rather than concentrating on what you do not have in your life. There are many benefits and important reasons for practicing this philosophy.

First and foremost, by sharing your gratitude with your heavenly support team, you are letting them know how much you appreciate the gifts, guidance, and love that they share with you. They love to hear this from you and they love it when you recognize their presence in your life.

Secondly, by focusing on what you do have—a good home, adorable pets, money in your bank account, a job you enjoy—you fill your heart with gladness for the souls, events, and creature comforts in your life, making it easier for you to recognize just how rich you really are in the things that truly matter to you. When you focus on the things you do not have, it creates a state of mind that is focused on lack, which is also referred to as poverty consciousness. By living in this mind-set, you may be subconsciously drawing more lack to you. When you view yourself as poor or lacking, you will be poor or lacking because you are sustaining that state of mind within yourself. For example, if you keep obsessing and thinking about what you do not have, such as money or a loving relationship, then your focus will be on that instead of the good you do have in your life. This type of thinking has the tendency to draw you down into a negative spiral of self-pity that is a waste of precious time and resources. If you are repeatedly thinking that you do not have money, you will not have it because your focus on the problem will sap your motivation to search for solutions. If you focus on the positive in your life and what you are grateful for, then you will draw in more beneficial experiences because you are appreciating all you have received and you know you are worthy of the abundance God intends for you.

Furthermore, if you place your trust in God and the angels to provide for your needs and heartfelt desires, they will do just that and then some. Please keep in mind that in order for good to come to you, you need to listen to what your heavenly support team is telling you, and then follow through with the instructions they provide for you. They will communicate with you using your intuition, daydreams, and external signs.

Allowing Your Heavenly Support Team to Guide You

When you consciously allow yourself to daydream, keep an open mind and allow ideas and thoughts to drift through your mind without trying to control or direct them. In this way, you will receive answers to your questions or solutions to issues that have been on your mind. Your intuition will tell you which ideas you should act upon. If you need help relaxing enough to allow ideas to flow freely, take a walk outside to clear your mind. Consciously make an effort to release the thoughts about your problems or concerns, and focus instead on the fresh air and the beauty of the world that surrounds you. Ideas will start to flow without your even realizing it. Allow them to grow on their own and enjoy the process of receiving solutions and ideas in this manner.

Additionally, listen to your intuition, which includes the gut feelings you have about your life path. If you have a very strong feeling that you should or should not take a particular action, it would be wise to heed that message, because it is direct guidance provided by your heavenly support team through your higher self. However, if that feeling is based in fear and anxiety, such as not wanting to attend a social outing because of a fear of meeting new people, then that is not your intuition speaking but the negative voice of your ego trying to prevent you from having an enjoyable time.

Pay attention to the external signs that may come to you in a variety of ways, such as through conversations that inadvertently provide you with a solution to a problem, or repetitive images or phrases that light the spark of your imagination toward finding a solution. Spirit orchestrates these wonderful opportunities for us. Our heavenly support teams love it when we recognize their efforts on our behalf, as it demonstrates our awareness and belief in the extraordinary connection that we share with them in spirit.

God's Plans

Keep in mind that God has a plan for you that may or may not match the vision you have of your future. In fact, most of the time, it is even better than any dream you have ever dreamt. Maintain an open outlook that allows you to trust in God and the angels to bring about your dreams in the best way possible. Let go of the strings that tie you to past disappointments and look for the good in your life at this moment in time. Concentrate on what you do have, express your gratitude, and trust that God and the angels are taking care of the manifestation of your dreams, prayers, and heartfelt desires.

Greeting the Day with Optimism

Each day brings us new opportunities to grow as souls. If we get stuck wishing for situations to be as they were in the past, we miss out on the opportunities of the present ... and the present is the only time we can make choices and take action. The past is done, the future is yet to be, and now is the time to act. Even though situations may not have turned out the way you would have liked, stand back and look at the positives of what you do have in your life.

Gratitude Exercise

As an exercise in gratitude and to see how easy it is to recognize, share, and feel the uplifting energy that flows through your spirit, concentrate on what you are grateful for right now. You can voice your gratitude out loud or to yourself or, better yet, write a list that you can refer to at a later date when you need to be reminded of the wonderful events, people, and circumstances in your life.

Think about the aspects of your life that are listed below. Allow yourself to feel the love and appreciation flowing through your heart and spirit for every moment, person, being, and event. Express gratitude for each and acknowledge how each has positively impacted your life:

- ♥ The relationships you have with the people around you, including acquaintances, friends, colleagues, neighbors, significant others, and family members

- ♥ Pets, animals, and nature (e.g., beautiful flowers, the sound of the ocean, walking through lush forests, the sun shining on your face, the full moon reflecting off of water, seeing double rainbows, finding a bird's nest, etc.)

- ♥ Who you are and the unique set of skills you bring to the world, as well as what you have achieved (both large and small victories)

- ♥ Your home, cherished belongings, and money you have earned or received as a gift

- ♥ Your jobs, career, or hobbies

- ♥ Your physical and emotional well-being

- ♥ Time (e.g., to enjoy with your children or someone special, to have to yourself, to do that which brings you joy, etc.)

- ♥ Events and accomplishments that have shaped your life and helped you to grow as a person

- ♥ The presence of God and your heavenly support team in your life

The list does not need to be confined to what I have above. Feel free to add your own items. The purpose of this exercise is to open the gateway of gratitude by helping you to see how many wonderful aspects there are to your life that are right in front of you.

Daily Recognition

It is a wonderful practice to share your gratitude on a daily basis with the universe, including your heavenly support team, people, animals, and nature. Appreciation can be expressed in words or with actions. For instance, you can tell someone how much you appreciate them, or you can show them by performing a task you know they will appreciate, such as cleaning up the house without being asked, arranging a day trip to their favorite place, making them a gift by hand, giving your pets a treat they love, or picking up litter to show Mother Nature how much you appreciate the beautiful bounty provided by the earth.

Feel the Joy

As you communicate your gratitude, allow your light to shine on everyone and everything around you. Most of all, feel the joy in your heart that comes from knowing that you are loved by God and the angels for being just who you are—a beautiful spirit and beloved child of God.

Embrace
the Love
within
Your Heart

Falling in Love with Your True Self

Would you marry you? I am not asking this to be coy but to ask if you would marry yourself as you would another, not just because you love yourself, but because you are *in love* with who you are as a person. And by that I mean, do you truly love who you are inside and out, including great qualities and flaws … as you do when you are in love with someone else? This is not about a puffed-up ego stating you are the greatest person in creation, but about having the joyful feeling of true love for yourself. Do you love who you are? Do you love every aspect of yourself, even your shortcomings? Do you forgive yourself when you have done wrong as you would another? Do you encourage yourself as you do others? Do you thank yourself and give gratitude to yourself for learning important lessons and being able to see the positive in situations that were challenging to handle?

Taking a Look at Your Inner Dialogue

When friends are upset or feeling down about relationship problems or mistakes they had made, do you berate them and make them feel worse about themselves? Or do you comfort them by helping them to see the positive actions they took and the silver lining or higher purpose for the events that took place? Most of us would lend an ear and provide kindness and understanding or apply well-meaning tough love based on an objective perspective of the situation. If we treat our friends in such a kind and understanding manner, why do our inner critics go into overdrive when we have problems or make mistakes? Why do we berate ourselves for the difficult circumstances we face instead of providing love and constructive feedback as we do for our closest friends?

Recognizing the Gift of You

Being your own worst critic is a demotivating tactic that comes from the fearful voice of your ego. This hurtful voice can be silenced with practice. I spent a number of years being very hard on myself until I learned how to appreciate who I am and all of the accomplishments I have achieved so far during my time here on earth. You, too, can learn how to see the beauty of your spirit and to value every aspect of you. It takes a conscious effort to turn your thought patterns around because negative thinking can become a habit. It pushes its way into our lives every day, but we can choose to deflect it and even step beyond the clouds that hover in order to see the light of our own souls.

A great way to start this shift in consciousness is to write a *Gift of Me* list highlighting all of your accomplishments and positive attributes. Sit in a quiet spot, place your hands over your heart, and take a deep breath in through your nose and exhale out through your mouth—find your center, which is a still place within you that is peaceful and without judgment. As you exhale, tell your ego to take a backseat and release all of the negativity that has built up within you. As you inhale, visualize positive energy flowing into your being and throughout your body. Dismiss all of your everyday concerns and focus on you and your heart. If you need help releasing your worries and cares, ask your angels for assistance. They will be delighted to help you with this task.

Breathe deeply at least three times. Then start thinking about you and your positive accomplishments, both planned and unplanned. Think about what you have done in your life and the kindnesses you have extended, as well as the moments that made you feel good about yourself. Write them on your list. Be honest. This list is for you, not anyone else. Keep the entire list positive. If any negative thoughts intrude, push the unwanted interference of your ego away and get back to your list. Once you really get going, I think you will be amazed at what your list reveals. Store your list in a special location where you can easily retrieve it.

From time to time, sad feelings or negativity may make cameo appearances in your life. If you are having a hard time setting those feelings and the ego's ranting aside, pull out your list to remind yourself of how wonderful your life really has been. Practice the breathing exercise to find your center. Keep your list growing by adding your accomplishments, both big and small, as well as positive life-altering events and moments that have brought you the most happiness and joy. Maintain your list like a well-tended garden that is fed with acknowledgment and appreciation for the gift that is you.

Unfortunate Events Do Serve a Purpose

Even though we are focusing on the positive, it is important to understand that adversity and seemingly negative events do serve a purpose. Situations that appear to be ruinous may actually be blessings in disguise, as it is sometimes necessary to remove from your life that which is no longer useful. You may balk at this at first; however, if you relax and be honest with yourself, you will see the higher purpose that the situation is serving. It may even lead to some of the more important and happier times in your life by clearing away harmful situations or by pushing you to go beyond your perceived limits in order to help you achieve your dreams.

Remember, without darkness, there would be no light. Problems arise when we let the darkness rule our lives and thoughts, making it seem as if negative experiences are the expected norm. They are not. All experiences can be learned from and utilized for good. By making a list of your accomplishments and positive attributes, you are giving yourself the opportunity to see and appreciate all of your life experiences and the gift of you.

Being Your Own Best Friend

Now that you have begun to recognize your wonderful attributes and accomplishments, it is time to start thinking of yourself as your own best friend. When you find yourself mentally and emotionally beating yourself up, stop and find your center. If necessary, pull out your Gift of

Me list to remind you of how wonderful you truly are, and then think about what you would do if your best friend was in a similar situation. Ask yourself what you would say to them or do for them and do that for yourself instead. Be kind and honest with yourself. Know that you did the best you could under the circumstances you faced and let go of the angst. Learn from your mistakes and commit yourself to doing better the next time you are confronted with a similar situation. Honestly assess the dilemma and determine the actions you took that did not provide the results you desired. That knowledge is invaluable, as it will help you to blaze new trails by trying out different solutions, move in a new direction, and open up new opportunities for you to grow.

Falling in Love

At a time when I was struggling with a relationship dilemma, I received a spirit medium reading from my friend, Valerie, in which my deceased father came through. He said, "You need to marry yourself first." When Valerie asked me if I understood what he meant by that statement, I said "yes." At the time, I thought it meant I had to love myself for who I was, but now I know that my father meant that I needed to *fall in love* with myself first.

We are constantly searching for love from outside of ourselves. During our search for love, companionship, and a sense of belonging, many of us often forget to turn our attention inward and unconditionally love ourselves. In actuality, a lack of self-love makes it more challenging for us to find and enter into satisfying relationships with others.

You can start falling in love with who you are by putting into practice the following positive affirmations and actions:

♥ Being kind to yourself

♥ Forgiving yourself for the mistakes you have made and learning from them

♥ Believing in yourself and your dreams

♥ Appreciating the unique gifts and talents you were born with and have developed over time

♥ Respecting yourself and honoring your boundaries by not doing anything that you do not want to do, and assertively speaking up for yourself in a calm and confident manner when facing people who are attempting to push you past your limits

♥ Knowing that you deserve the best, and opening your heart and spirit to receive it

♥ Doing what brings you the greatest joy

♥ Giving yourself time to play and rest

♥ Sharing your gifts, talents, and love with people who respect and honor you

♥ Releasing negative thoughts, fears, and worries about yourself and others

♥ Being honest with yourself and others

♥ Recognizing and acknowledging the light and beauty that is you

When you truly love yourself, your spirit is filled with tremendous joy that brightens your light in this world. As your light grows, it reaches out and touches the souls of others. We are all connected in spirit, and when your light shines with such brilliance, people cannot help but to be drawn to the beautiful luminescence that is your soul. Most importantly, you are acknowledging God's incredible love for you. The bond you have with your Creator becomes much more intimate as you begin to understand just how wondrous the exchange and intertwining of love really is between you and all of creation.

All Other Relationships

Once you have truly established a loving relationship with yourself and God, all other relationships will follow because you will be at peace with who you really are, both internally and externally. Fear of not finding or receiving love will disappear, because you already will have it within your own heart. Other people will see and recognize the inner peace and contentment within you, which naturally draws them toward the true light of your spirit that is radiating out to the world. Moreover, when you are in harmony with yourself, it is easier to share your heart and joy with others. At the same time, it is easier for you to accept love from others because you know you are worthy of receiving gracious gifts and abundance from the universe.

♥

Be True to Yourself

Once you have fallen in love with your divine self, you will find it much easier to make decisions that are in accordance with your deepest desires and dreams. Respecting yourself and honoring who you are becomes a way of life. You are more likely to listen to your heart and intuition because you have established a level of trust with yourself and God that enables you to tune in to the guidance that comes from the depths of your own soul, as well as from your heavenly support team.

Each day, we make numerous decisions that affect our life paths and the evolution of our souls. The choices may seem insignificant, such as where we go to get a cup of coffee, or significant, such as deciding to take a leap of faith and follow our dreams. Each decision we make, whether large or small, plays a part in our destinies. If you remain true to yourself by listening to what your heart and intuition tells you, you allow yourself to be guided by your soul's inner knowledge of your life path and you allow divine guidance to step in to help you to move forward on the path your soul is destined to take in this lifetime.

What does your soul urge you to do? What actions can you take to be true to yourself while sharing light and love with others? Once you have answered these questions for yourself, follow through with actions that are in keeping with what you truly desire in your heart.

Advice from Well-Meaning Loved Ones— Who Should You Listen To?

Keep in mind that there are many well-meaning people in the world who dispense all kinds of advice to you about your life. They could be best friends, mothers, fathers, acquaintances, or even co-workers. While it is good to listen to them and glean nuggets of advice, ultimately it is up to you to listen to your heart as to which path you should take. Does their advice have a ring of truth to it that resonates with your desires, or does it bring on a negative or uncomfortable feeling? If you are unsure as to which way you should turn, you can ask your angels and God for guidance, as they are always eager to help guide you on your path. Our heavenly support teams speak to us through our intuition and our hearts. They send us signs every day. You can consciously open yourself to their guidance and ask for their assistance at any time. To focus on one particular question, try this exercise called *Finding Your Center*.

Finding Your Center and Asking for Guidance

Place your hands over your heart and breathe deeply—in through your nose and out through your mouth. As you inhale, envision positive energies entering your body and as you exhale, envision negative energies exiting your body. Take at least three to five deep breaths. Concentrate on breathing and clearing your mind of all extraneous thoughts. The rhythm of your breathing should sound like the waves of the ocean. As calm washes over your body, physically feel your focus shift from your mind to your heart. Ask God or the angels your question and wait for your answer to come through to you. The answer may come to you in a variety of ways; it all depends on which of your senses is most dominant. For instance, you may see a vision with your third eye, or you may hear the answer come to you in your own voice or theirs. Do not dismiss anything you see, hear, feel, taste, smell, or suddenly know, such as a particular thought or epiphany. Jot down notes about what you have observed because your answer is contained within. If you do not receive an answer right away, do not worry. Your heavenly support team has heard you, and they will provide the answer for you in the coming days through external signs, dreams, and your intuition.

If you have a strong feeling that you should take a certain path, then do it, as long as it is based in love. Any answer you receive that is not in harmony with the love of the universe is your ego getting in the way; it is not the angels or God. They would never tell you to do something that is harmful to you or others, nor would they tell you to do something that is not in accordance with your true self. Therefore, if the annoying chatter of your ego tries to get in the way by instilling fear or worry, tell it to take a backseat and readjust your focus back to your heart. Take those deep breaths, center yourself, and restate your question.

After you have received your answer, visualize the positive outcome of your choices as already perfectly manifested and acknowledged by your spirit. The next step is to take the necessary actions to bring your dreams to fruition with the guidance you receive from your heavenly support team through your heart and intuition.

Have Faith in You

You know what rings true for you. You really do know what feels right, especially if it is an important decision you need to make. Your decision may seem contrary to what other people think you should do; however, those people are not living your life, you are. Therefore, stay true to you.

God has a plan for each one of us, and if we listen to the messages of our hearts that are sent to us by our heavenly support teams, then we can most closely follow the plans we established for the evolvement of our souls prior to being born on this earth.

Let your unique light shine with the glory that is you!

♥

Balancing Giving and Receiving

The balancing of energies is intrinsic to our souls. When you look at our world, there are many examples of polarities, such as night and day, masculine and feminine energies, and oceans and deserts. It was created in this way to ensure that all elements remain in balance, with the energy of one available to offset the energy of the other. For example, extended dry weather conditions cause a drought and too much rain causes flooding, both of which can have a strong impact to life on earth.

The same is true for all aspects of our lives—too much work drains our spirits of enjoyment and too much play keeps us from fulfilling our life purposes. Balance is important to maintain harmony within our own spirits, as well as with those around us. When we are giving too much or taking too much in our relationships, the balance is upset, which can lead to resentment, a feeling of being drained or taken advantage of, feelings of guilt, and depression.

An Over-Abundance of Generosity

In the case of giving too much in any relationship, the person who is excessively giving will eventually run out of energy and motivation to provide such a generous bounty. Over time, resentment can build to unprecedented levels. If you are in a situation in which you find yourself being overly generous and you feel your needs are not being met, you can help yourself by addressing the issue with the person or persons involved.

Calmly and courteously express your needs, define what you need to receive back in the situation or relationship, and ask the other party if they are willing to make an effort to restore the balance in your relationship. Give them some time to learn how to make the adjustment, because it may not happen overnight. They may not have been aware of the deficit, and if you do not speak up for yourself, they may not ever be conscious of the pain they caused.

If you are a person who primarily gives, it is important to love and respect who you are, and to learn how to speak up for yourself. Your needs are relevant, too. There are people out there who will take advantage of you if you let them. Some will have sob stories they will tell you to get you to feel sorry for them. Do not fall for it. Standing up for yourself can act as a wake-up call to the people who were not aware that their behavior was detrimental to you. It can open the door to improvements in your relationships, as long as each person is ready to commit to making positive changes. If changes are not forthcoming and sustained, then it may be more beneficial for you to remove the people from your life who want to drain you of all of your resources. These people can be friends, family members, colleagues, clients, spouses, significant others, or acquaintances.

In addition, it is important to respect your feelings and learn how to say no. If someone asks you to do something and in your heart you know you really do not want to do it, but are tempted to say yes only to please the other person, you should not do it. You do not need to give a reason or excuses for saying no. Just say, "No, but thanks for asking me." What you choose to do is your prerogative. Know, too, that you are not required to give up all of your love, time, money, or more for someone else. That is too much for anyone to expect from you. The other person must be willing to meet you at least halfway. A perfect balance of giving and receiving is difficult to achieve or maintain; however, efforts need to be made by both parties to work on maintaining the relationship. If the person you are involved with does not want to restore the balance of giving and receiving, and continues to take from you without regard for your feelings, then it may be time to end that particular relationship, whether it is professional, familial, friendly, or romantic.

To restore the balance within yourself, learn how to be receptive to gifts and abundance. Know that you are a beautiful soul that is worthy of receiving blessings. Open your heart, mind, and soul to receiving blessings without guilt or a feeling of obligation to return the favor every time one comes your way. Expressing gratitude is sometimes all that is needed to graciously thank the giver of a gift. By learning to receive, as well as give, you will restore the balance within your spirit to healthy and harmonious levels.

An Over-Abundance of Taking

In the case of taking too much in a relationship, the person who is excessively taking may eventually feel a strong sense of guilt. The side effect of that guilt can be depression and pointed avoidance of the person they have been depending upon. To restore the balance before it gets to this stage, the person who is displaying this behavior needs to think about what he or she can offer to the person or persons involved. If you have not been giving back in your relationship, think of what the other person would appreciate and do that without him or her having to ask for it. Make sure it is something they will truly appreciate and not something you are doing in your own self-interest. If you are unsure of what to do, ask. Take the time to talk with the person or persons involved, acknowledge the deficit your behavior created, and find out directly from them what you can do to repair the balance in your relationship. Be sure to follow through in a timely manner on what you have promised. It will go a long way toward rebuilding the trust and restoring the balance in your relationship. As you move forward, make concerted efforts to continue to give, as well as receive.

Another way to learn how to become more giving is to volunteer your time to charities and people in need. In this way, you will see firsthand how important it is to be generous with others. To restore the balance within yourself, give what you would like to receive, such as love, time, money, or something else meaningful to you. In time, you will feel better about who you are and balance will be restored within your spirit.

If you are primarily a person who takes more than you give, it is important to love and respect who you are, and to learn how to provide for your own needs. Continually taking from others indicates a strong level of dependency that shows a lack of respect for yourself and others. Learn how to stand on your own feet and give without expecting in return. Do not fret or allow anxious thoughts to sidetrack your progress. You can do it. The balance you achieve in your relationships and the independence you discover within yourself will build your self-esteem and enable you to have healthy, loving associations with others.

Personal Experience—Lessons Learned with Al

Years ago, my best friend, Al, was greatly dependent upon others. Al did not want to get a job or take responsibility for himself, even though he was more than capable of doing just that. Instead, he depended upon others for his income and his needs. Eventually, he drained the resources and patience of all of his friends. When he was losing his place to live once again, he came to me asking me to take him in. I said "no." I did not say that out of meanness, but out of kindness. I knew if I took Al in, I would only be feeding into his dependency upon others. Even though it was hard for me to deny my best friend a place to live, I did so because I was concerned for Al's spiritual well-being.

Closing the Door on Dependency

Instead of opening my home to Al, I did offer to drive him back to his foster parents' home more than five hours away. The days and nights leading up to our departure were challenging. Al was upset with me, but I stood strong. He needed help breaking his pattern of co-dependency, and I had to remain steadfast if he was to succeed. I did not want to lose Al as a friend; however, I knew that re-establishing his self-respect and love for himself were more important than any pain I would feel if our relationship ended.

The night before we left, he was saying just how independent he was, how proud he was of taking care of his life all on his own, and more along that vein. Needless to say, I could not believe the words coming out of his mouth. He was in complete denial, which is not uncommon for able people who heavily rely on others to take care of them. I knew he was very upset with me for not taking him in; however, I also knew I could not and would not take on a dependent—especially not one who was more than capable of taking care of himself. Feeding his dependency would have destroyed our relationship without fixing the problems Al faced. I knew that if I allowed him to become dependent on me, I would have become resentful and he would have sunk down deeper into despair.

The Challenges That Come with Administering Tough Love

The drive to his foster parents' house was calm. Music played on the radio as we engaged in casual conversation. There was no more talk of independence, only discussion about the town he was returning to after years of being away. After I dropped Al off with his foster parents, we continued to write to one another, but I could tell he was very resentful. After a while the letters slowed but did not stop. He had obtained a job at a local fast-food restaurant and really disliked living so far from his friends. One day, Al called me to tell me he was truly independent now. He had saved his money and wanted to return to where his friends lived. He asked if he could stay with me for two weeks while he looked for a job and a place to live. I was wary of inviting Al into my home because I was not entirely convinced that in less than six months he had completely turned his life around. For that reason I answered that he could, but on the condition that he understood that at the end of two weeks, if he did not have a job or a place to live, he would need to move on. This is what I call tough love. I was willing to help Al out for a short time, but if I did not put a limit on it, he would fall back into his old ways and end up as a permanent, and dependent, resident in my house.

Al agreed to my terms; however, I do not think he thought I would enforce them. I am glad I set them in place because his next question was, "When can you pick me up?" He asked as though he lived only fifteen minutes away instead of five hours. I kindly mentioned that if he was so independent, he would find his own way back to the area by going to the bus station and buying a ticket. I told him I would be glad to pick him up from the depot when he arrived in the area.

Al did get on the bus, and he did stay at my house for those two weeks. Unfortunately, all he did was sleep and watch television all day. He did not bother to look for a job or a place to live. He gave me excuse after excuse as to why he was not taking any action. I reminded him that his two weeks were quickly coming to an end and that he and his belongings would need to be out of the house by the designated date. It may sound heartless to you that I could throw my best friend out on the street; however, I would have been performing a great injustice to both of us if I had allowed him to stay. It was difficult to be that strong. I knew I had to be, though, for both our sakes.

Down to the Wire

The day before he was supposed to leave, he still had not found anywhere to work or live. I pulled out the area phone directory and started calling places for him to stay as he sat right next to me. I found a few options for him and told him it was up to him to follow up. When I came home the next day, lo and behold, Al had found a boarding house about a mile and a half away, as well as a job within blocks of where he was staying! Hallelujah! When push came to shove, Al came through for himself!

An Amazing Turnaround

After working for a few months, Al had saved up enough money to get his own apartment. He was in his forties, and it was the very first time he had an apartment of his own. He was so proud! He did it all on his own!

Bittersweet

I will say that Al did resent me for several months, even after he had established himself in his own apartment. I knew from the start that this was the price I might have to pay. The loss of friendship was hard for both of us, as our relationship had cooled to the level of acquaintances. I loved him very much and hoped that one day he would understand why I had to take the steps I did in order to help him stop his dependency upon others.

Time Really Does Heal All Wounds

We did renew our friendship in time and Al did appreciate his newfound respect for himself. He even experienced a wonderful reunion with his birth mother and his siblings after more than thirty years of separation.

An Important Message from Heaven

Soon after Al and I renewed our friendship, God decided it was time for Al to cross over into heaven. Years later, I received a message from Al that came through during a spirit medium reading. He came through to tell me that he was incredibly grateful for all I had done for him. He understood why I had stood strong and risked our friendship. He was very appreciative of the independence he had achieved, as well as the self-esteem and self-love he had gained from the experience. The wash of love he sent to me was absolutely amazing. It brings tears of joy to my eyes even now, as I feel his love coming through. Al always was and always will be a special friend to me. He certainly knew how to bring a smile to my face and, even now, he continues to do the same by sending me a message from heaven. As I finish writing this paragraph, he is sharing with me his great happiness and pride that his story is being shared in a way that has the potential to help others. He is grateful that the lesson he learned keeps on giving. He hopes you, too, will learn from seeing how loving and respecting yourself, whether you have historically been known to excessively give or take, can reset the balance within your own spirit, as well as within the relationships you have with the ones you love.

From Al's spirit to yours and from my spirit to yours—Namaste!

♥

Knowing You Are Not Alone on Your Journey through Life

Have you ever felt as though you are all alone in this world, facing the challenges of life? I have felt that in my lifetime, especially when I was going through a particularly tough time. It felt as though there was no one around who understood what I was going through or who could be there for me to listen or to provide comfort. I have learned that throughout my trials and tribulations, as well as my joyful experiences, I have never truly been alone—and neither are you. You have a support system in heaven that comes from our Creator, the angels, your spirit guides, past spiritual masters, and deceased loved ones. They are there for you. They see your struggles and worries. They hear your prayers. They feel your pain and want to ease it for you. They also share your joy and happiness. In essence, they are there for you in good times and in bad.

The Roles of Your Heavenly Support Team

Each and every one of us has a heavenly support team. It is good to know who is working with you and who to thank when you know you have been helped. For that reason, I would like to provide a brief introduction to the main members of your team, as well as the services they perform in your honor.

The Archangels

There are many different orders of angels. One order in particular has been tasked with directly aiding humankind—the archangels. Whenever you pray for their help, you are, at the same time, praying for help from God, our Creator. Likewise, when you share your gratitude for their love and assistance, you are also sharing your gratitude with God.

The archangels[1], such as Michael, Gabriel, and Raphael, are all-seeing. They are very familiar with our individual soul plans, as well as those for the entire planet. They are never too busy to help any one of us with anything we feel we need help with, as they can be in many places at once. One of their jobs is to serve God by assisting us with the evolvement of our souls. They directly oversee the *Hall of Records*, which is where all of the documentation about our souls is stored. The records are referred to as the *Akashic Records*.

Spirit Guides

We are all born with at least one spirit guide that accompanies us throughout our entire lives. Spirit guides are spiritual souls that have dedicated themselves to facilitating the soul plans of spirits on human journeys. They prompt us along our paths of soul evolution. Throughout your life, you may have additional spirit guides who make cameo appearances in order to guide you with specific projects or life lessons. You can get to know your spirit guides through meditation.

---

1   As a note, Doreen Virtue's book *Archangels 101: How to Connect Closely with Archangels Michael, Raphael, Gabriel, Uriel, and Others for Healing, Protection, and Guidance* is a great source for learning about the archangels.

Past Spiritual Masters

Past spiritual masters are highly spiritual souls who have served here on earth as human beings on a spiritual journey. Examples of past spiritual masters include Buddha, the saints, Jesus, medicine men and women, gurus, shamans, and more. They offer us specific help in their areas of expertise when we ask for it and often make an appearance in our lives when we need a reminder of their teachings. Depending upon the spiritual or religious background in which you were raised, you will most likely gravitate toward past spiritual masters who are associated with your upbringing. However, you can be introduced to new past spiritual masters through education exploration of the various religious and spiritual beliefs throughout the world. Pay attention to which teachings resonate within your heart, as these may be clues to the past spiritual masters who are assisting you with your life and soul evolution.

Guardian Angels

Guardian angels are souls who are in heaven and have volunteered to watch over you. Many of them are people you have known in life, such as parents, friends, or godparents. They can also be people you have never met in this lifetime, but who have a close association with you, such as a great-grandparent or a member of your soul group who has opted to stay behind in heaven. In many cases, guardian angels are members of our immediate soul groups. They like to visit us to see how we are doing. Many young children can see them and often talk with them … many of those imaginary friends are not so imaginary after all!

The range of their power is limited, though, to the knowledge that they have about your life. They can produce miracles for you with the help of the archangels. For instance, many people exclaim that they must have had a guardian angel watching over them when they narrowly escaped an accident. Often, this is the case. Angels do step in to prevent catastrophes that could potentially interfere with your life plan. Not everything is predetermined before we are reborn on earth and sometimes a little help from your angels prevents a turn of fate that would take you off course from your spiritual goals.

Deceased Loved Ones

Our deceased loved ones support us from heaven with their love. They visit us in our dreams, as well as in our waking hours, to let us know they are nearby. Many of them volunteer to be our guardian angels. Others take on additional roles that support us in our lives. For instance, my grandfather, affectionately referred to as "Pop-Pop," elected to help me with my mediumship work. In his most recent lifetime, he was unable to fulfill his dream of openly communicating with spirit. In heaven, his dreams are being realized and in a manner that exceeds his expectations. One of his jobs is to organize and handle the details for the readings that I provide through communications with your deceased loved ones. Your loved ones visit him to facilitate appointments with me. They then prompt you through external signs, messages, and circumstances to visit me for a reading. It is amazing how spirit organizes all of these events. He takes great joy in being able to assist in this manner from heaven ... and he does an amazing job, too! Thanks, Pop-Pop!

Asking for Guidance and Assistance

Your heavenly support team is there for you whenever you need them. They will not step in to assist you without being asked or receiving your permission to help unless it is a dire emergency. This is because we have been given the gift of free will. We have to choose whether we are going to trust our heavenly support teams to support us and whether we will openly accept their guidance, divine intervention, and gifts of abundance.

Please note that just because you ask for something, it does not mean it will be bestowed upon you or, if it is, it will be bestowed upon you right away. Our heavenly support teams see more than we do and know if what we are asking for will do us more harm than good. If that is the case, then they will answer your prayers in a different way and with something better than you had even imagined. Remember to listen and look for their guidance to come to you through your intuition, daydreams, ideas, epiphanies, and external signs. Practicing meditation and the Finding Your Center exercise are great ways to connect with your team and its guidance, as it is at these times that the chatter of the ego, which tends to block heavenly communications, is quieted.

If you are in tune with your metaphysical gifts, you can use the Finding Your Center exercise to directly reach out to and receive messages from your heavenly support team. If they are silent when you ask for help or guidance, it may be because there is a life lesson to be learned and they are not to interfere with the next steps you are to take in your life. Your heavenly support team is there for you and watching over you from heaven at all times. If you need reassurance of their loving presence, ask them for a sign that they are near. The sign may come in the form of a symbol that has a positive meaning for you, or it could be the finding of a coin or feather, which indicates that your deceased loved ones or angels are around.

♥

Reaching Out to
Your Heavenly Support Team

You can reach out to your heavenly support team at any time through prayer, in thoughts, or in writing. Ask them for help with a situation you are facing. They hear you and will do what they can to answer your prayers and requests for assistance, as long are they are in accordance with your soul plan and the greater good. If what you are praying for or asking for will ultimately cause you greater sadness and pain, or send you down a path that will do more harm than good, your heavenly support team will do their best to guide you toward better opportunities that meet your true needs and desires. For example, if you are praying for the return of a lost love and that person does not return right away, it may seem as though your prayers or requests are not being heard or answered. They have been answered—just not in the way you may have expected.

Patience Works in Your Favor

Sometimes it takes time for prayers or requests for help to be answered. The timing is not based on what we think is best, but on the perfect timing

64

for the evolution of our souls. Sometimes, too, we may not get what we asked for because there is something better coming along for us. Even though we may not always recognize the assistance that is materializing from our heavenly support teams, we can help ourselves by having patience and an open mind about how our prayers will be answered.

With the situation involving a lost love, God and the angels know that what you are really asking for is someone who will love and appreciate you for who you are. The person whose return you are praying for may not be ready to do that at the time of your prayer, or there may be lessons each of you still need to learn before progress can be made. It could also be that you were only meant to be together to learn specific soul lessons, and now it is time for you to part ways and move on to relationships that better suit your needs. Or, the timing may be perfect for your souls to reunite and the person will return to you. The possibilities are endless, and only heaven really knows the various paths we will take. They are written in the Akashic Records that are stored in heaven. The Akashic Records are a compilation of all that was, is, and will be for each of our souls.

We can assist our heavenly support teams in the answering of our prayers and requests for assistance by being mindful about our actions and expectations, as well as by looking at our experiences to see what lessons we need to learn from them. In addition, we need to learn how to trust in the heavenly guidance we receive and have faith that our heavenly support teams are working on our behalf. By taking responsibility for our thoughts, actions, and beliefs, we are actively participating in the evolutionary process of our souls.

Know That You Have Been Heard

Keep in mind that our support teams in heaven see and know much more than we do here on earth. They know everything about us and what would be best for the evolution of our souls. Therefore, when you ask for help, know that they are working on your behalf and that they send you their love. They are always there for you when you need them. It is as simple as reaching out to them through your thoughts and prayers, knowing full well that your heart's desires have been heard and will be answered at the perfect time for you. In the meantime, find your center, be at peace with yourself, and know that you are accompanied on your life's journey by heaven's finest representatives who fully support you, your dreams, and the evolution of your soul.

Handling Situations That Test Your Faith

Many times in my life, I have experienced situations that have greatly tested my faith. I am not patient by nature; however, I have found that through the endurance of uncertain, stressful, and challenging situations, I have learned to cultivate an inner peace with the help of God and the angels. Their presence in my life blankets me with comfort and love, as well as a sense of knowing that everything is going to work out even better than I think. It is an amazing feeling to have that faith and love flowing through your entire being. It comes from knowing with all of your heart that events will turn out in the best way possible if you put your trust and faith in God and your heavenly support team.

Temporary Losses of Faith

My own inner peace comes from my absolute trust and faith in God and the angels. I know that they are actively working on my behalf to manifest my dreams. As a spiritual being on a human journey that is subjected to the persistent babbling of the ego, I sometimes need to remind myself of that trust and faith. Even Mother Theresa questioned her faith from time to time. According to a *Time Magazine* article published on August 23, 2007, Mother Theresa stated that she suffered a crisis of faith for almost forty years because she did not feel the presence of God.[2] God was there for her, though. In fact, he and the angels never left her. Mother Theresa, like many others, continued to persevere with the work of her calling despite her feelings of absence brought on by the negative voice of the ego because, deep in her heart, she knew God was supporting her.

I have found that when I feel as though God's presence has slipped away from me, it is because I am living through a life lesson that requires me to make a decision about my faith and the course my life will take. During those times I know that God and the angels are there, even though they are silent. That silence can feel like a great void that may be disturbingly unsettling—that is, until you realize that they are waiting for you to make decisions regarding your fate and faith. It is important to note that the periods when I temporarily lose my faith are getting shorter and shorter because I am teaching myself to recognize and dismiss the grief and fear that comes from the ego. When the moments of weakness appear, I specifically ask for, and gratefully accept, the help of my heavenly support team. They may respond to my plea with silence, not because they have abandoned me, but because of the life lesson I need to learn on my own using my free will. I know they have my best interests at heart and want to help me to live the best life I can live with the most happiness. God and the angels want

---

2   David Van Biema, "Mother Theresa's Crisis of Faith," *Time Magazine,* August 23, 2007, http://www.time.com/time/magazine/article/0,9171,1655720,00.html.

the same for you. Ask for their assistance and be sure to generously thank them for their presence in your life, as well as for their loving guidance.

Building Your Relationships with Your Heavenly Support Team

To begin building trust within your relationships with God and the angels, start by asking them to assist you in small ways, such as finding a parking spot or locating the perfect product to fit a specific need while shopping in a store. It may sound frivolous and funny; however, by asking for help with the small things, you will gradually learn to feel more comfortable about asking for help with matters that are of greater importance to you.

As your level of comfort increases, you will notice that not every whim and desire is answered on an immediate basis. God and the angels work on their timeline, which may be very different from your own expectations. Know that they have heard your prayers and requests. They will fulfill them if they are beneficial to your life path. When you trust in their judgment and do not try to force situations to turn out the way you would like, you are opening up the doorway to an abundance of positive possibilities. Your dreams will come true, and your experience in life will be better than you have ever imagined. This has happened in my own life, and it can happen in yours as well.

The Magic of Being in Tune

I have seen dreams from my childhood and beyond unfold before my very eyes, dreams that I have held close to my heart for years. At various times in my life, I had dreamed of becoming a psychologist, of becoming famous by working on film and the stage, of becoming a published author, and of being a spirit medium. Each of these dreams have either come true or are in the process of coming true, but in different ways than I had imagined.

Paging Doctor Hluchan

My dream of becoming a psychologist was based on a desire to assist people with emotionally-based obstacles and issues. This dream of helping people through communication and understanding has come true through my gifts of mediumship, which allow me to provide healing messages from your heavenly support team. Throughout my life, I have always carefully observed human behavior, my own and others', and have strived to understand the motives behind behaviors and how best to deal with the situations we encounter in life. It is interesting to note that due to the insight and advice I shared with people, friends and co-workers tended to joke around and call me "Doctor Hluchan" (pronounced *loo-chin*). At the time this began, I did not realize that the information coming to me was being provided by my higher self and my heavenly support team. To this day, there are people who refer to me as "Doctor Hluchan," which I take as a wonderful compliment and evidence of the healing that transpires when I share my gifts with others.

Setting the Stage

Little did I know that the work I used to do on stage and film as a professional actress, as well as the hundreds of presentations I prepared and delivered in my career as a marketing manager and in college, were in preparation for services I provide today as a medium. By performing and delivering presentations in front of large groups of people, I tamed my stage fright. This is very important for the readings I give because fear can block me from receiving messages from spirit. My dream of working on stage in front of large groups of people has come true through the large group demonstrations and spirit medium readings I provide. Even though my purpose for being on stage is definitively different from my original childhood dream of being an actress, by following that dream in my youth, I was able to prepare myself for the level of comfort required for the public presentations and readings I provide today.

It Is Written

My dream of becoming a published author is coming alive with this very book you hold in your hands. In high school and for a portion of my college education, I was an English major. Writing has always come easily to me; however, all of the books I started to write were never completed ... until this one. All of my experiences with writing have been applied to almost every job I have held in my life. Because of this, I have continually improved my skills and now use them to complete *How Have You Loved?*

Reawakening to My Gifts

As for my dream of being a medium, I did not realize I was one all along. I had seen spirits, felt them, and heard them; however, I thought that in order to be a medium, I had to see them fully manifested as "ghosts" all of the time. Events facilitated by spirit led me to the knowledge I needed about my gifts of mediumship. During an angel reading I received from my friend, Joshua, an incredible awareness and recognition of my gifts lit up my mind, and suddenly I understood the reason for all of my life experiences. Each moment had led me to this reawakening, and I was able to see that I had been communicating with spirit all along. Later that evening as I was getting ready to go to sleep, I thanked God and the angels for reawakening me to my gifts. As I did this, I was blessed with a fantastic sensory experience that opened my mind to the great expanse of the universe. I knew without a doubt that everything good that I believed about the universe and our life purposes was true, and that there was so much more to life than I had ever imagined. Starting the very next day, events began to unfold at lightning speed. Once I had truly acknowledged my gifts, it was as though I had unlocked a door in my mind to the knowledge that had been there all along.

The Path Reveals Wonders

The path that led me to the fruition of my dreams did not always seem to be straight, but in actuality it was, because there were very specific experiences I needed to go through that were building the skills, trust, and faith I needed for my dreams to materialize. As you can see, my dreams are coming true and in a way that exceeds my expectations.

The good news is that there is more to come. That is why patience, trust, and faith are necessary. You may not clearly see the road ahead, but they do, and your heavenly support team is constantly working toward helping you achieve your dreams.

When it comes to dealing with situations that do not seem to be supportive of your dreams, it is a good idea to take a step back and try to view the situation from a different perspective. Remember, at the time a situation is unfolding, we may not see where we are being led. An unusual or seemingly negative situation may actually be a blessing in disguise. Let it be okay with you that you are not steering the ship. Trust that every experience, whether positive or negative, is an integral stepping stone that is leading you toward your ultimate happiness and the fulfillment of your dreams.

You Are in Control of You and Only You

It is essential to keep in mind that you are in full control of how you react to situations and people. That is the only thing you are in control of—your actions or reactions to the environment around you. When a seemingly negative event occurs, you can choose to let the negativity take over your psyche, you can opt to take it in stride, or you can learn from it and decide to move forward with your life.

When I encounter challenging situations, I ask God and the angels to help me to elevate my thoughts and to understand how the circumstances fit into my soul plan. I have felt their peace descend upon me in such a way that it feels as though a physical cloak of comforting energy was wrapped around me. Whenever I feel my confidence or trust waver, I remind myself that God and the angels are looking out for me and my loved ones. Often, I will ask the angels to infuse the situation and the people involved with love, which I visualize in my mind as the great white light of the Creator interspersed with the soft, warm, pink glow of loving energy. Likewise, you can ask the angels to assist you and your loved ones and to heal the situation in a manner that benefits all concerned. I often ask the angels to be by my loved ones' sides when they are going through a particularly challenging time and to lend their loving strength and guidance as it is needed. You can do the same for you and your loved ones by sending the angels your requests through your thoughts and prayers.

Most of all, do your best to remain calm and remind yourself that every circumstance you encounter is an important step in the evolution of your soul and in the realization of your dreams.

Living with Absolute Faith in Your Dreams

It is amazing how absolute faith provides an inner peace and a level of calm and acceptance that everything is going to work out in the best way possible for you. It means believing that God and the angels have your back. They are listening to your heartfelt prayers and dreams, and are working toward manifesting them for you in this lifetime.

There are messages and signs all around us and, most of all, there is proof of our dreams coming true. I recently had many uplifting experiences that were direct answers to my prayers. I received these gifts because of the love I have for myself, as well as for my heavenly support team. By knowing that I am worthy of receiving wonderful gifts and abundance, I consciously choose to be open and receptive to the guidance and love I receive from heaven. On a regular basis, I specifically ask for, and willingly accept, assistance from my heavenly support team. I continually strive to release negative and distrustful thoughts in order to establish absolute trust and faith that spirit in heaven is working on my behalf.

Actively working on uplifting my thoughts is a practice I embrace every day. There are times when I experience moments of doubt. It is in those moments that I turn to God and the angels to help me to elevate my thinking to see beyond the moment, to accept with grace the delays that are occurring, and to instill peace and acceptance of the circumstances that caused the doubt to surface. In order to do my part, I meditate and employ the Finding Your Center exercise to release the angst and usher in my inner peace.

We Are All Worthy

Abundant gifts and love from heaven are available to you. We are all the perfect children of God. This is not a religious statement, but a spiritual statement. I am not the first person to say that God resides within us, as us, and I will not be the last. The Creator is very much a part of each one of us, which means our thoughts and prayers are in direct communion with God and the angels.

The angels and God want me to share this message with you because they want you to know that everyone has the opportunity to receive divine assistance from heaven. Every single one of us is worthy. All we have to do is believe with absolute faith and trust that the gifts of heaven will come into our lives with perfect timing.

Demonstrating His Love and Power

This may all sound a bit unbelievable to people who have experienced a significant amount of setbacks and disappointments in their lives. However, I can tell you from personal experience that I have worked hard to overcome the obstacles I have faced from both inner turmoil and external situations. It is possible to see and experience the light of God's love, regardless of the circumstances you face. Others of you will read these statements and will readily believe and know that your heavenly support team is there for you.

God will show you his love and power, especially when you have absolute faith. Those that dismiss this message are not to be looked down upon. They have not yet reached the place in their lives where they can take that leap of faith to believe in the unseen. That is their choice, and it should be accepted as such. My prayer is that they will someday soon embrace the absolute faith that delivers gifts from heaven. If they do not see it or experience it in this lifetime, they will certainly see it, know it, and believe it once they reach heaven, because it is at that time that the veil that covered our knowledge of the divine is removed, revealing truths to our souls.

We have the power and ability to remove that veil while we are here on earth through our connection with heaven. Not everyone will reach that point in this lifetime, however, but many have and many will. Say a prayer for the people who do not see and experience the light of God. Do not pity them, though. Send them kindness and love instead, while keeping in mind that we are all on different levels of learning and soul evolvement. In another lifetime, you may have been where they are, and they may have learned lessons that you have not yet comprehended in this lifetime.

Setbacks Are Temporary

Know that your faith will be tested from time to time by trying circumstances. This is because you are human, and part of being human is the existence of the counterproductive voice of the ego. A setback is as temporary as you want it to be, as you are in control of your thought processes. If you find yourself falling into negative or nonproductive thinking, stop. Find your center and express gratitude for something in your immediate environment. Participate in an activity that brings you joy. This will help you to elevate your thoughts and stop the negative running commentary. You can also ask your heavenly support team for assistance with the elevation of your thoughts. Once your thought processes have transformed and you are fully embracing your faith, those circumstances will no longer hold the same grip on you. As you make peace with yourself and your circumstances, a sense of calm and acceptance will descend upon you, which will enable you to maintain a more positive outlook on life and to flex with the unexpected situations that crop up in your day-to-day experiences.

Use Common Sense When It Comes to Medical Issues

It is important to note that, while I have absolute faith, I do believe that when there are medical problems, it is important to visit a doctor. Doctors, nurses, and medical practitioners are here on earth to assist us with our health. When I go to the doctor, I pray to receive the best care possible, and I thank God when I do because God works through everyone. We are here to help one another. We all have a positive purpose to serve. Use common sense when it comes to medical issues and know that God guides the hands of professional healers.

Believe That Your Dreams Can Come True

Your dreams can come true. Have faith, watch for the signs, and listen to your intuition. Follow through with what your intuition tells you because it provides you with guidance that comes through your spirit from heaven. If negative thoughts get in your way, practice the Finding Your Center exercise. Believe with all of your heart that your dreams can come true … and they will with time, patience, absolute trust, and absolute faith. Therefore, when you dream, dream big and with a confidence that matches your true heart's desires. You may find that God's plan for you is even better than what you had ever imagined!

The Gifts of

Mediumship

What Happens When We Cross Over into Heaven?

Through my communications with spirit, I have been given wonderful insights regarding what happens to our spirits when our physical bodies expire here on earth.

Every soul is given the opportunity to cross over into heaven. Our way is lit by an incredible white light that is almost blinding in its brilliance and shimmers with facets of rainbow colors on the outer edges. Heavenly delegates, which can include deceased loved ones, angels, spirit guides, and past spiritual masters, are there to greet us and to guide us as we journey to heaven.

Once we have crossed, the veil is lifted and we are once again reunited with the knowledge and understanding that may have eluded us while we were in human form. We review our lives in a nonjudgmental way to see how our souls progressed on their earthly journey. It is at this time that we are asked the question: "How have you loved?" Forgiveness, healing, and compassion are extended to us as we explore and understand the reasons we acted the way we did and the choices we made, including how we gave and received love.

Our souls continue to evolve while in heaven but in a more joyous way. We learn new skills, volunteer for jobs and special assignments, and learn to exist within the peace and harmony that surrounds us as we await our reunions with members of our soul groups—our families, friends, and loved ones—who have yet to cross over. Some may choose to come back to earth for more lessons; however, most choose to wait for the reunions with their most intimate soul groups before coming back again.

Healing in Heaven

The only unnatural type of death is suicide. All other forms of passing, including accidents, murders, and diseases, are natural ways for the physical body to expire because they occur when God decides it is time for a soul to return to him. As a result of religious teachings, some people believe that those who commit suicide are condemned to torture in purgatory or a wretched existence in hell. Souls on earth who, in great sadness and desperation, take their own lives are given the opportunity to cross over into heaven. However, it is up to the soul to decide whether it will cross over into the heavenly paradise that awaits them. Due to feelings of inadequacy or shame, some souls may not believe that they belong in heaven. When a soul rejects his or her opportunity to go to heaven, the gateway for entry will eventually close. This leaves the soul stuck between two worlds, which can be very frustrating. The only torture that occurs comes from within the soul itself. Despair about not being in heaven and not living with a physical body on earth, weigh heavily on the soul. He or she may try to communicate with loved ones who are living on earth; however, unless the person on the receiving end of the communication is in tune with his or her metaphysical gifts, the efforts will most likely fail. All is not lost, though, as a soul in this situation can cross over into heaven with assistance from God and the angels. The soul must be willing to accept that help in order for the transition into heaven to occur. After they have crossed, they will be reunited with their loved ones who have crossed over before them.

My best friend, Michele, was one of those souls who took her own life, as was my Aunt Eileen. I know from my communications with Michele and Eileen, as well as with others who have taken their own lives, that those who commit suicide are all given the opportunity to return home to the arms of God. I will say, though, that the experience is not what they might have expected. Had they known in advance, they may not have chosen to end their lives in this premature manner.

Once these souls realize the damage they have done to themselves and the evolution of their souls by taking their own lives, they experience a wrenching despair that resonates throughout their entire spirit. During their life review, they are given glimpses of what could have been if they had just hung in there or had made different choices throughout their lives. Instead of a joyous reunion with loved ones who have already crossed over, the reunion is more somber, as the occasion is bittersweet. There is no party or celebration as there would be with a natural death, because there is a tremendous amount of spiritual pain that must be healed when these troubled souls realize the extent of what they have lost out on by interrupting their souls' carefully planned evolvement through life on earth. To assist them with the healing they need, these souls move forward to a place in heaven that I refer to as a *spiritual hospital*. Help is given to them at the spiritual hospital for as long as it takes and, when they are ready, they are able to rejoin the rest of the population in heaven for more pleasurable reunions with loved ones in spirit, continued soul growth, and exploration of our heavenly paradise.

The lessons and soul plan that they cut short will need to be repeated. The second time, though, they will have the benefit of the additional healing and instruction that they received at the spiritual hospital, which, if heeded, will make their paths easier and will help them to more readily recognize the light of their own spirits. Through the recognition of angelic assistance, they have the opportunity to be guided and assisted to a more satisfying life on earth and the completion of the soul plans that they cut short out of great despair.

As a note, Michele received the healing she needed. She is enjoying her time in heaven and has been assisting me for more than two decades with my psychic, mediumship, and intuitive work. Thanks, Michele! I am glad you received the guidance and assistance you needed to heal your spirit.

As for Eileen, she has been reunited with her loved ones in heaven and is receiving the help she needs at the spiritual hospital. In time, she will be able to enjoy the full privileges of great peace, serenity, and joy that are granted to us upon our return to our heavenly paradise. Bless you, Eileen, for making the choice to cross over into heaven, which is where you, like all of us, belong.

The Spiritual Hospital Is Open to All Who Are in Need

As an extension of its services, the spiritual hospital helps those who need to heal from the hurt they received or dispensed during their lifetimes on earth. Peace, understanding, and counseling are offered to work through the issues that caused pain and suffering for the self or others. Sometimes, these issues were part of a soul contract. Other times, they were caused by the soul's refusal to see the light and learn the spiritual lessons that were decided upon prior to birth. No matter what the circumstances were that surrounded the issues, healing is offered and opportunities to learn and do better the next time abound.

Additionally, the spiritual hospital helps those who need help waking up. My grandmother, affectionately known as "Mom-Mom," who suffered from Alzheimer's before her passing, came through with a message saying that it took her a long time to wake up in heaven after her physical body had expired. People who suffer from Alzheimer's or other comatose conditions enter into a dream-like dimension that I refer to as *heaven's waiting room*. While there, they relive the positive memories from their pasts, receive visits from the angels and loved ones who are in heaven, and get a chance to play and be free. When their physical bodies expire, they are not always aware that they have officially crossed over into heaven. This phenomenon requires them to receive assistance with waking up to the realization that they have now fully come home to heaven. The resident angels of the spiritual hospital administer gentle prompting and reminders at a pace the soul can handle.

On a side note, people on earth that enter a coma-like state or have a near-death experience (NDE) also spend time in heaven's waiting room. Their experience is similar to the experiences of people whose bodies have permanently entered into a catatonic condition. Often, when people reawaken from a coma or an NDE on earth, their lives are forever changed by their experiences. On an immediate level, there is a sense of peace and calm that rests within their souls because of the glimpses they had of heaven. This may also be accompanied by a feeling of elation or great joy. Those feelings may or may not last long. It all depends on the person and whether or not they believe that what they saw and experienced was real. Sadly, some souls dismiss the experience as a dream and nothing more. Others may be upset that they have returned to life on earth. Those that recognize the profoundness of the experience are enlightened by their knowledge and, as a result, tend to appreciate the life they are living here on earth in a much more spiritual way.

We Choose Whether or Not We Go to Heaven

Ultimately, we choose whether or not we want to travel through the gateway to heaven. We all have free will, even when it comes to a decision such as that. Most souls choose to cross over; however, there are some that do not, possibly as a result of fear, doubt, or confusion. There are many reasons people choose not to cross over into heaven. Some souls fear that others will not survive without them, they may doubt where they are being led, or they may be confused about the fact that they are no longer in human form. Others may believe that they do not deserve to be in heaven due to their actions on earth. This does not mean that the gateway to heaven is forever closed to them. Once their particular gateway closes, these souls will need assistance with their crossing, such as an opening provided when someone else crosses, assistance from the angels, or with the help of a medium who opens the gateway and calls in the angels. Until assistance arrives, they reside in spirit between worlds, which some religions refer to as purgatory. It is not hell, as hell does not exist in the sense that was taught by our religious predecessors.

It can be confusing and upsetting for souls who are not in heaven and not on earth. Because of that, they may use their energy to break items and cause a disturbance. They are not mad at you, but rather are frustrated at their situation and are trying desperately to get your attention. They do not understand why they are stuck or how to resolve the problem. As a note, there is a distinct difference in the feeling that comes from spirits who have crossed compared to ones who have not crossed. Spirits in heaven emit a joyful and uplifting feeling, while spirits who have not crossed tend to emit a heavy, negative feeling that reflects the sadness of their situations. If you suspect that you have a spirit such as this around you, it is best to contact a medium who can help this soul cross over into the light.

The Existence of Heaven

One of the most important messages that God and the angels want you to understand is that heaven does exist. They want you to take comfort in knowing that your spirit continues on after your body ceases to exist here on earth. Moreover, they urge you to live well and love during your time here on earth, knowing that all of your experiences here are for the evolution of your soul and that your heavenly support team will help your spirit in its transition to your next destination—heaven.

Coping with the Loss of a Loved One

When loved ones cross over into heaven, it can be a painful emotional experience for those who are left behind. We grieve because we miss the physical closeness of the person or pet whose presence made a difference in our lives. Even though they remain connected to us in spirit, it can be challenging to cope with the changes to our daily living. In essence, our loved ones are continuing on a spiritual journey that we cannot take with them because we are meant to stay here on earth and fulfill our own life purposes.

The feelings of loss can be devastating and heart-wrenching. Trying to continue on with our lives may be problematic as grief threatens to overwhelm our emotional well-being. Grief is a natural feeling that accompanies loss; however, grief can be lessened with knowledge. Knowing that our spirits do not die with our physical bodies lessens the pain of physical separation from our loved ones and changes our perceptions of the finality of death.

The Four Stages of the Grieving Process

There are typically four stages of the grieving process that we may experience before or after a close loved one or pet passes on. As you go through the process, you may move forward or backward through the stages due to intense emotional reactions to the changes you are facing.

- ❤ The first stage includes shock, disbelief, or denial.

- ❤ The second stage involves anger toward the person, life, God, yourself, or others.

- ❤ In the third stage, you acknowledge within yourself that the death has occurred or will be occurring in the future, as is the case with someone who is terminally ill. In addition, you recognize the inevitability of the change you are facing, as well as your own inability to alter the circumstances. These thoughts may be accompanied by sadness or a feeling of emptiness or numbness that can be attributed to the loss you are experiencing.

- ❤ In the fourth stage, you achieve a level of acceptance and peace about the transition your loved one has made or will be making into heaven. Understanding and forgiveness are extended for the manner of the death and for the anger you held in your heart during the second stage.

It is important to note that the stages of grief can begin before a loved one's physical life on this earth has ended. When a person is terminally ill, the grieving process may be experienced while his or her spirit resides on this earth in its physical body. Stage one may occur with receipt of the news of the terminal illness. This may be quickly followed by the second stage, in which anger takes over. The third stage may bring about deep depression for the person who is suffering from the illness, as well as for their loved ones who are watching their passing in what seems to be slow motion. Depending upon the person and the circumstances, the fourth stage may be reached prior to the actual passing of the person. When this happens, the passing itself is seen as a relief because the person who has passed is no longer suffering with the pain of a debilitating illness, injury, or disease.

Connected Through the Heart of Our Spirits

We all have the ability to give and receive messages from our loved ones, as we all are born with at least a touch of the gifts that allow us to communicate with one another through our spirits. This works both here on earth, as well as with spirits in heaven. We are all connected through the heart of our spirits, which is how we truly communicate with one another, whether we are consciously aware of that connection or not.

Spirits in heaven hear your thoughts and prayers. They also see the letters and notes you write to them, as well as the poems you compose with them in mind. Do not worry if you have had thoughts that have been less than happy about your loved ones, as they understand that we are human and may not have the understanding, knowledge, or perspective that comes to us when the veil that separates us from heaven is lifted.

Spirits send messages to you through your sense of sight, hearing, feeling, smell, taste, and intuition. I am amazed every day with the communications that come through from spirits. As a spirit medium, I know that it is not residual energy from a person or pet who was here on earth, but an actual transmission of information in real time. Spirits show me what they are doing in heaven, whether it is reuniting with loved ones who have already crossed over or engaging in activities that bring them happiness. In addition, they bring forth messages and advice that pertain to your life and the lives of your loved ones on earth.

Continual Growth and Contributions

Learning and evolving as a soul continues in heaven. The lessons we learn there are different from the ones we learn here on earth. This is because the environment is completely different. On earth, there is a lot of negativity and harder lessons to learn. The speed at which our souls evolve is much faster here on earth due to the challenging circumstances we face. In heaven, we thoughtfully review the lives we have lived in order to determine the lessons we have learned and still need to learn. We embrace the knowledge that was veiled from us on earth with compassion and understanding for ourselves and others. Anxiety is a thing of the past. Spirits have communicated to me that our time in heaven is not just for rest and joyful reunions, but also for making considerable contributions to all spirits through meaningful jobs that assist those in heaven and on earth.

Children in Heaven

Through the communications I have received from spirits in heaven, I have seen deceased loved ones caring for children who have crossed over. These children continue to learn, grow, and play in heaven, surrounded by the love and affection of the angels and spirits of those who have crossed over before us. When the time comes for the children to be reunited with members of their families, they will initially appear as family members remember them. This is so that the spirit within you can readily recognize the spirit of the child who has crossed over before you.

Enriching and Satisfying Activities

There is an infinite number of jobs our deceased loved ones can perform. Some of them include providing assistance with the orientation process for souls who are returning to heaven, working with the earth's elements and environmental conditions, and energy healing work. Deceased loved ones who are especially skilled in specific fields may elect to be muses for musicians, writers, artists, architects, engineers, scientists, doctors, mathematicians, and more. They lend their personal expertise to souls on earth by sharing inspirational ideas and solutions from heaven. They work in collaboration with other experts residing in heaven, including the angels. All of our inventions and ideas originate in heaven and are passed to us through epiphanies, intuitive thought transmissions, daydreams, and dreams. It is through similar collective consciousness transmissions that we also share thoughts, ideas, and feelings with one another on earth. We tap into this great storehouse of information consciously and subconsciously when we are looking for answers, solutions, and fresh inspiration.

In addition to technical and creative jobs, many of our deceased loved ones volunteer to be guardian angels in order to protectively watch over us and our loved ones. It brings them great comfort and joy to bear witness to the unfolding of our lives and dreams. Most importantly, the jobs our deceased loved ones choose to perform are the ones that bring them the most pleasure and happiness.

Our Spirits Continue to Shine

We can take comfort in knowing that death is not the end, but a new beginning. It is the next phase of our journey and evolvement as souls. For those here on earth, the connection of the heart that our loved ones have with us never dies because our spirits live on. Besides our own beautiful spirits, we do take our love and relationships with us when we travel onward to heaven. When people comment that "you can't take it with you," they are right when it comes to money and possessions. However, you can and do take with you the most precious and important aspects of your spirit—your love and the heartfelt connections that you have with the people and animals you have loved while living on this earth.

Accepting and Flowing with New Beginnings

When confronted with the loss of a loved one, take comfort in knowing that their spirit lives on in heaven and that, when the designated time of your passing arrives, you will be reunited with them. In the meantime, we have our own soul evolvement to attend to on earth, including learning how to release the grief of physical separation and to move forward with our lives by taking comfort in the love that resides in the heart of our spirits. Part of living our lives here on earth is learning how to cope with loss. We can either let it consume us and eat away at our happiness, or we can choose to accept that endings are truly new beginnings for us and our loved ones, whether on earth or in heaven.

When I come across people who are struggling to cope with the loss of a loved one here on earth, I extend great compassion. I understand what it means to physically lose someone you love. At the same time, I provide comfort to them through the messages I share from their loved ones. The transformation that occurs in this healing process is amazing. The light of God's love touches the souls of the people I provide readings for, and it is always my hope and prayer that they will remember the feelings and the messages they received. Most of the time, people do move forward with the proof they have received from their loved ones that they are happy in heaven. At other times, I have seen people remain at peace for a week or two and then descend back into a deep gloom that has covered them for years. This is their choice. It may be because of feelings of guilt or even anger that a loved one is no longer here in the physical sense. Counseling may be required to help people in this situation to learn how to forgive themselves and others, as well as to understand that God does not punish us by taking away our loved ones. When the physical bodies of our loved ones expire due to natural causes, it is their time to return to heaven according to the timing that was determined prior to their birth on earth.

Pets and Animals Go to Heaven, Too!

Pets and animals go to heaven. They, like us, have beautiful spirits that are housed within their physical bodies while on earth. It is a wonderful comfort to know that we will be reunited with them in heaven. Many of them like to be there to greet you when it is your time to cross over, especially if you had a deep connection with them. You will see your pets as they were when they were at their best—youthful, healthy, and happy. I often joke about the menagerie that is going to greet me when I return to heaven. People who know me well know I enjoy the special connection I have with the animals, birds, reptiles, fish, and insects of this earth. They are amazing spirits that bring light to this world and teach us many important lessons.

Enjoying the Delights in Heaven

Animals enjoy the same delights of heaven as people. They can run and play and be young again. They can volunteer to perform jobs that assist souls in heaven or on earth, or they can opt to enjoy their time engaging in their favorite activities in their heavenly paradise. Any pain or diseases they suffered from in life are gone. In much the same way that our deceased loved ones look after our children who cross over, they also provide care and love for our pets and animals. I have had many pets come through in readings to let their loved ones know they are happy and grateful for the loving relationships they shared with them. Do not be surprised if you feel their presence next to you as you lie down to go to bed or while sitting on the couch. You may feel a depression in the bed or couch where they are resting next to you in spirit, as well as a sensation of warmth that represents their love for you. I have experienced this several times, as have several people for whom I have provided readings. Your pets in spirit love to snuggle up with you from time to time to let you know they are there and continue to share their love with you.

Messages from Our Animal Friends in Heaven

When I am giving a spirit medium reading, it is such a delight when pets come through. Their love and joy bursts with such purity of emotion. Pets are incredibly excited to share their love with you. When they enter a reading, I usually feel their presence in the same way that I sense human spirits who have crossed over in which males come in on my left and females on my right. I sense the shape of their bodies as they were when they were on earth, and I feel the warmth of their love radiating from their spirits. At the same time, I may be receiving images or flashes of color or fur type (or feathers, scales, or skin) to help identify what they looked like when they resided here. Dogs of mixed breeding send lightning-quick flashes of the breeds that make up their backgrounds. On the heels of those images, I hear the sounds they made in life, such as purring, yipping, or chirping. Once they have identified themselves and you have recognized who they are, they send me love and feelings to share with you. This exchange of information occurs in the same way that a spirit that was in human form communicates with me—through impressions of emotions, thoughts, and visions. Some of you may be wondering how thoughts come through in a manner I can comprehend. A good analogy would be that it works in the same way as the United Nations meetings; it is as though I have a pair of headphones on that instantly interpret the communication into English. This happens when I receive messages from any spirit that communicates in a language other than the ones I have learned while residing here on earth. It is truly an amazing experience to behold.

No Need to Be Sad

Although we often feel sadness when a person's or a pet's life ends here on earth, we can take comfort in knowing that they are going to a very happy and peaceful place. The spirits of all living beings exist beyond life on earth to enjoy the abundance and grace of heaven.

♥

How You Can Prepare for a Spirit Reading with a Medium

Going to see a spirit medium for a reading is an exciting prospect. For the uninitiated, it can elicit a feeling of nervousness or even fear of the unknown. Rest assured, communication from spirit is a miraculous phenomenon that allows us a means for transmitting and receiving messages to and from our heavenly counterparts. I am constantly in awe at this fabulous form of communication. No matter how many times I perform readings, I always experience a great feeling of gratitude for the ability to bring healing and comfort to the souls for whom I provide messages.

Messages of Love

Any spirit that comes through for you during a reading is not there to berate you or to bring up topics in an effort to embarrass or hurt you. They are there to ease the pain of your heart by sending you their love, to provide you with closure regarding their whereabouts, to ease your mind about the existence of heaven, and to provide guidance with regard to the life you are now living. At no time have I ever had anyone come through that had anything but loving words and advice to share. You see, once we ascend to heaven, the petty disagreements we had on earth fall away. We gain understanding and knowledge, and learn the true purpose of our experiences when the veil is removed. Grudges, anger, and fear no longer take hold of our spirits or block out the positive experiences we were meant to encounter. Heaven is a wondrous place where peace and love prevail. Therefore, look forward to the messages you are to receive and approach the reading with an open mind and heart. The natural excitement that comes from receiving the gift of messages from heaven can bring about healing in a manner that is better than you could have ever imagined.

The Importance of Keeping an Open Mind

I frequently tell people to keep an open mind when it comes to being the recipient of a reading. I ask this not only of you, but also of myself. The more open I am, the clearer the messages I receive. Preconceived ideas about who will be coming through and the messages they want to share can block receptivity to the spirits who are actually coming through. The more open you are not only to the messages, but also to who is coming through for you, the better your reading will be. When you concentrate too hard on wanting a particular person to come through, you may not recognize or hear the actual spirit who is coming through. It may not be your child or your husband, but your aunt or grandparents.

This is not because those in spirit that you would like to hear from do not love you. They do love you very much; however, it could be that the time is not right for their message to you or that someone else has a message you need to hear first. Sometimes, certain beings come through first in order to assist others who need help communicating with a medium. It is important to keep in mind that the messenger is as important as the message itself. Spirit knows who you need to hear a message from and why. Moreover, certain deceased loved ones may have waited a very long time to get a message to you.

It is very important to note that I do not command spirits. Like those of us on earth, they are gifted with free will. They choose whether or not it is beneficial for them to appear. At times, when a certain deceased loved one is mentioned by the recipient of a reading, they may pop into my consciousness and share a message; however, I cannot command spirits to come. It is not my job to try to override the plans of heaven. I have full trust, as should you, in their knowledge and understanding of you and this world in which we reside. They certainly do have a bird's-eye view of what is going on with our lives that we do not typically have here on earth. Therefore, my best advice is to keep an open mind. You may be secretly hoping and wishing for particular loved ones to come through; it is certainly understandable. I have done it myself in the past when I was receiving a reading; however, I was also able to accept the fact that if someone did not come through, there was a good reason for it, whether it was timing or that a more important message needed to come through from someone else.

Cooperative Effort

Communication that utilizes the gifts of mediumship is a cooperative effort. If I have someone sitting across from me with their arms crossed or if they have formulated in their mind that they are only going to believe that spirit is really there if the medium shares a code word from their loved one, there is a strong possibility that they will be disappointed. People who sit with their arms crossed are consciously or subconsciously trying to block energy. Furthermore, having your arms crossed is a physical posture that indicates discomfort, anger, or dislike regarding a situation. People who become fixated on hearing a code word or specific phrase are trying to force spirits to do their bidding, which is not how a free exchange of information works. A request such as this usually comes from a non-believer or skeptic who does not understand the light, the free will of the spirit, or the intricacies of spirit communication. Remember, the only spirit we control is our own that is now housed within our own bodies. I do not control you, you do not control me, and neither of us controls spirits in heaven. That is how the gift of free will works. We are all in control of our own destinies and actions at all times, even after we have made the transition into heaven.

On the opposite end of the spectrum, if I have someone sitting across from me who is relaxed and open to the gift of this blessed form of communication, they tend to be more receptive to the messages coming through. Even excitement is good, because it raises the energy level in the room. It takes a lot of energy to do the work I do, because spirit on earth and spirit in heaven operate on different vibrational frequencies. I need to raise my energy level and spirit in heaven needs to slow theirs down in order for us to meet somewhere in the middle. Extra positive energy in the room is always a bonus and certainly provides a cooperative and welcoming atmosphere for this unique communication exchange. Moreover, by cooperatively adding your energy to the reading, you are helping your loved ones as they work to express their feelings and thoughts with you.

The Validation Process

Once I have opened up my aura and energies, spiritual beings will begin sending me information about themselves in a variety of ways, including but not limited to images, sounds, thoughts, physical indicators, and emotions. This portion of your reading is called the validation process. What the spirits are doing is sending through information that will help you to recognize their identity. They may indicate to me the manner of their death, physical characteristics, personality traits, the type of relationship they had with you while on earth, or a number of other indicators that will help you to recognize them. It is your job to listen to the information in order to correctly identify who is coming through with a message for you. As I share the information with you, I may ask you if this resonates with you or if the information makes sense to you. Try to limit your answers to "yes," "no," and "I don't know." This request is for your benefit. If you feed me too much information, you may not entirely believe it is your loved one coming through. Both the spirits and I want you to walk away from your reading knowing it was them and not information you inadvertently shared with me.

That said, I do know that when loved ones in spirit are recognized, memories and excitement arise. I understand this, and so does spirit. Do not worry if you forget to keep your answers to "yes," "no," or "I don't know." Sometimes it is appropriate to share your memories, as it will help you to process the messages you are receiving. Spirit will let me know if I need to gently ask you to stop sharing in order for them to do their job. In essence, do your best to keep your answers short. If you forget, it is not a big deal because spirit will let me know when it is appropriate for you to share more information or not. On a side note, it is important to clarify that there are times when I may ask you a question that requires a more detailed response. It is acceptable to respond to that question with honesty. An example may be when a spirit is trying to transmit details to me regarding a disease that contributed to their passing. I can explain the physical indicators and symptoms that you recognize, but I may not know the exact name of the disease. I may ask you for the name of the disease in order to add it to my databank of memories, which will assist me with future readings if other beings come through with the same ailment or symptoms.

The Message

Once the identity of the spirit is recognized and acknowledged, I ask them what their message is for you. You will most likely not hear me ask this of the spirit out loud. As an interesting side note, as I am receiving information from spirits, processing it, and sharing it with you, I am simultaneously asking spirits questions to draw out even more information for you and the purpose for their visit. It is a fascinating process involving multiple exchanges of information occurring at a rapid-fire rate. The messages they share vary greatly; however, they do carry one very important theme—love. The very act of participating in this type of communication is based in love—your love for them, their love for you, and my love for all spirits, as well as for being able to provide healing as a messenger of heavenly communications.

Tasks for You

I recommend that you take notes with pen and paper when you have a reading. The information that you receive can have a significant impact on your life, and you will want to remember it. Not all mediums allow audio or video recording devices; therefore, it is always good to ask before you record. Even if you do have permission to record, I still recommend taking notes the old-fashioned way because the energy from spirits may interrupt or interfere with the recording. They often like to play with electronic devices because electricity is one of the easiest forms of energy for them to manipulate.

Readings in a Group Setting

For group readings, the dynamic gets much more interesting. The more people there are in attendance, the more interesting the dynamic and the more challenging for the medium. Not to worry, though, the spirits coming through will send unique information to identify themselves to you. I will say again that it always amazes me how they work out all of the details before you even sit down for your readings. They have already decided who is coming through first, as well as the messages that they would like to share with you and the group. It is a very orderly and impressive process that is assisted in part by various beings, such as spirit guides, angels, and past spiritual masters.

There Is a Reason You Are Together

I would also like to note that when you are in a group setting, there is a reason all of you have come together at that particular time to receive messages from spirits. Even though not everyone may receive a direct message from a spirit, there is information that will be shared throughout the group event that will provide knowledge about heaven that opens the door to the healing process for you. For example, in a room full of twenty people, there may be three unrelated people who have lost loved ones in separate car accidents. When one of the spirits of these loved ones come through, the information they share may give comfort to the other two people who are not receiving a direct message. In the case of an accident involving a mode of transportation, I have often been informed by spirits that a person's spirit was removed from his or her physical body by the angels upon impact, eliminating the opportunity for pain to be experienced during the process of physical death. This is very comforting news for those loved ones on earth who have been imagining the potential suffering that their loved one may have experienced. In other instances, the experience of the reading itself and seeing how spirits communicate brings about a feeling of peace through the awareness of the reality of heaven, and the continuation of our spirits after our lives on earth. Each experience is personal for individuals that are in attendance. One of the most important gifts that they receive, though, is the love that is shared by spirits, as well as deeper insights into the inner workings of heaven and the purposes of our lives on earth.

Remembrances

It is helpful to have a friend or relative sitting beside you because he or she can help you to identify the loved ones that are coming through for you. Many times, the message that comes through could be of benefit to both of you. It is also good to have someone there who can assist you by taking notes while you are receiving a direct reading. I find this to be very helpful because when people are receiving a direct message from a spirit, their entire attention is focused on receiving that message, not on taking notes about all of the aspects of the reading.

Topics Covered by Spirit at the Beginning of a Reading

In addition to direct messages, spirits and angels provide information at the beginning of all of the readings I provide that is pertinent to everyone in attendance. I do not prepare what I am going to say in advance because the spirits and angels provide me with the topics that I need to cover for the people who are in front of me. One of the topics that comes up may be a very unusual phenomenon called psychic amnesia. This is an event that occurs when people who are receiving a reading forget information that they would usually remember or know. While attending a large mediumship demonstration, there was a man who was receiving a direct message from a spirit. The medium brought up the topic of this man's barn and his horses. The man responded that he did not know what the medium was talking about. From what it sounded like on my end, the man did not have a barn and horses. The medium continued on with the reading when suddenly the man piped up and said, "Yes, that happened when I went out to the barn this morning to feed my horses." The people in the room could not help but let out a short giggle because this man, only two minutes prior, had completely forgotten he even had a barn and horses! I am not 100 percent sure why this phenomenon occurs (it could be a matter of being nervous or in awe), but believe me, it does happen and it can be very challenging for the medium trying to share a message. You may suddenly find yourself having issues identifying deceased loved ones or understanding the meaning of a particular message or symbol that particular spirits are sharing with you. I tell people not to worry about it if this occurs. Write down all of the information that comes through in a reading as this will help you decipher at a later time who was coming through, as well as the messages they were sharing with you.

Clear Identification and Claiming Your Loved Ones

When spirit is coming through, it is important for you to do two things. One, try not to make the description fit a particular person you want to hear from. It is either them or it is not. Spirit will be providing you with information that is unique to them and your relationship with them. Two, speak up. If you are participating in a group reading and you think that a particular spirit may be one of yours, claim them. Even if you need more clarifying information to be sure it is them, it is better to speak up than to remain silent. Spirits will provide additional detailed information; however, if you do not claim a particular spirit as the one that belongs to you, the message will not be given. I make it very clear to both spirits and the recipients of readings that I will not pass along a direct message until the particular spiritual being has been clearly identified and matched to the loved one with whom they would like to share a message. This is because the message will have less of an impact or have less meaning if you do not know whom the message is for, as well as whom it is coming from.

Spirit Activity Immediately Before and After a Reading

Spirit knows before you do when you are going to have a spirit medium reading. In the weeks before or immediately following your reading, you may experience some light paranormal activity in your home, your car, or at work. There is nothing to be frightened of, as this is your loved ones in spirit letting you know they are around. Activity may include pictures knocked askew or even off of a wall or table; light bulbs that blink or blow out; a noteworthy appearance of butterflies, hummingbirds, ladybugs, or dragonflies; electronic appliances that act up; and external signs or reminders that bring to mind a particular loved one who has passed away. All of this activity is not meant to frighten you. Spirits do this to let you know that they are dropping in to say hello. The general feelings that can accompany these events are happiness, peace, and love.

Spirits Who Have Not Crossed Over into Heaven

As I explained previously, if you are experiencing paranormal events in which items move or break with no logical explanation, such as doors slamming or vases breaking, it may indicate that you have a spirit in your environment who has not crossed over. Individuals who have not crossed over are not mad or angry with you but with the situation of not being in heaven and not being on earth. As with human beings who are frustrated or confused, spirits such as these are looking for love and understanding. They may not understand why or how they became stuck between dimensions, and they need assistance in order to cross over into heaven. Yelling at them and telling them to leave will not make them go; it will only add more negativity to a frustrating situation. They would leave if they could. It is best to extend compassion and to contact an experienced medium who will help this individual cross over into the light.

Gratitude

As a medium, I am grateful to be a facilitator and a witness to the healing of spirit that occurs. It is an honor and a blessing to be able to share my gifts with you because being the recipient of a spirit medium reading is an extraordinary opportunity for you to receive information about your life, your loved ones, and heaven, as well as comfort, peace, and love.

As your reading comes to a close, it is a lovely practice to thank spirits for honoring you with their presence and for the delivery of their love and messages. I do so every time I give a reading or receive information from them. They are grateful for your gratitude and the acknowledgement of the efforts that it took to make this unique form of communication possible. Know that they thank you, too, for being open to such an incredible gift.

How Spirit Communicates
with Mediums

Many people that I meet have questions about how I communicate with spirits. Some of them are under the impression that it is only a straightforward conversation with a spirit or a video provided by spirits that tells me everything I need to know. This is not the case. Even though portions of the communications come across that way, most of it is much more complex than that.

Spirits communicate with me through a series of images, feelings, physical indicators, thoughts, tastes, smells, outward signs, instant knowledge, and in countless other ways. I explain to the recipients of my spirit medium readings that the information I receive is like an abstract puzzle that needs to be pieced together. Each medium's experience is unique. There are some similarities and there are some differences as to how we receive and communicate the information that is provided to us by spirits. The following is a synopsis of how it all works for me.

Opening the Communication Channels with Heaven

The process of giving a reading involves a fascinating, high-speed blend of information that needs to be quickly recognized, decoded, and interpreted. To begin the process, I concentrate on opening up my mind, heart, body, spirit, and aura to the light. This serves to heighten my receptivity to spirit communication through an extraordinary activation of all of my senses and raises my energy level to meet that of spirit. The connection is then made with spirit through the supreme source of love that flows throughout all beings. Immediately before I begin a reading, I express gratitude to the spirits for their participation and assistance with the messages that are about to come through, as well as for the blessing they are giving to all of us who are participating in this divine communication exchange.

After working with spiritual beings day after day, it is not necessary for me to formally open up my energy to communicate with them. My channels are continually open and running in the background as I go throughout my day, like an Internet connection that is always on but not always in use. I enjoy my connection with heaven because it reminds me that we are all connected to one another through our spirits. By keeping my channels open, I am increasing my receptivity to the multitude of external signs and internal messages that spirit shares with me about my life. I refer to it as being *in tune*.

The Importance of Grounding

Even though my channels are open in the background, it is important for you to understand that I do keep myself grounded when I am not in the process of providing a reading. To ground means to reconnect your spirit with your physical body. When I provide spirit medium readings, I raise my vibration level in order to communicate with spirits in heaven who vibrate at a faster rate of energy. In doing so, the energy of my spirit rises slightly above that of my physical body. If I do not ground myself, then I am slightly disconnected from the events occurring around me. While this is good during a reading because it allows me to concentrate on my communications with heaven and allows spirit to step into my energy space, it is not good when I need to concentrate on events occurring on earth. When I forget to ground myself, I have a tendency to lose or misplace items, such as my car keys or glasses, and I may experience some minor trouble remembering words or names. When this happens, I know that I need to consciously ground myself.

There are many ways to ground yourself. One way is to stand with your palms facing down toward the earth. Imagine golden roots growing out of your feet and down into the earth, about nine feet down. As the roots touch down, take a deep breath and thank Mother Earth for keeping you grounded. Take another deep breath and feel your energy stabilize within your body. Stand in this manner for as long as you feel it is necessary—between one and five minutes. When you feel a peaceful calm descend upon you, you have successfully grounded your spirit. Visualize the roots reversing their growth and drawing back into your feet. Other ways to ground include walking barefoot on the grass, working with the earth through gardening, and consuming root vegetables, such as potatoes, carrots, beets, onions, or parsnips.

It is interesting to note that many of the people I meet who have strong gifts of mediumship of which they are unaware tend to be smokers. There may be several reasons for this; however, two of them may be that they are unconsciously grounding themselves through the use of tobacco or that they are self-medicating the stress they feel from the onslaught of other people's emotions and moods, which they pick up on in their daily lives. In the latter case, people with strong empathic abilities may not be aware of how to protect themselves from absorbing the energies of others. If this sounds like you, a good way to protect yourself is by using the daily exercises that I discuss in the clairsentience section of the next chapter, "Receiving Messages from Spirit through Our Senses."

While tobacco can be used as a grounding method, it is not recommended for obvious health reasons. I recommend using the non-smoking and non-eating methods of grounding in favor of the ones that require the consumption of tobacco or food.

Deciphering the Code

As I progress through a reading, I focus on the task of accurately receiving, interpreting, and sharing the information transferred to me by spirit. First and foremost, I need to determine who is coming through and their relationship to you, as well as the specific messages that spirit wants to share with you. The ultimate purpose of spirits coming through is to provide you with healing, whether that is in the form of reassurance that they are in heaven, guidance about your life, or the sharing of love.

Spirits use symbols, imagery, sounds, aromas, tastes, thoughts, and feelings that I have stored within my memory, also known as my databank. Since my databank of experiences is unique to me, symbols, sounds, and images that come through for me may have an entirely different meaning for another medium. For example, during a reading, I was sent an image of a car that was the make and model of a car my father owned in the 1980s. The car I saw was medium brown (my father's had been light blue), and it was parked on a paved road that ran through a field of summer wheat. There was a young tree under which the car was parked. As I was receiving this image, I was hearing "1980" in my mind. I shared the descriptions of the images and the date with the recipient of the reading. As she was taking notes about what I said, I was getting an image of a young woman with brown hair, as well as the feeling of her presence next to me. After providing a description of her physical attributes and personality traits, my client acknowledged that the woman was a relative who had passed in 1980. Instantly, all of the information I had been sent made sense. The year of her passing was represented by the car. The brown was for the color of her hair. The wheat was displaying the time of year when she passed—summertime. The field looked like the one in the cemetery where my best friend was buried. As the images rapidly flickered through my mind again, additional information was being provided by this young woman in spirit. All of a sudden, I knew that this young woman had passed away in the same manner as my best friend, Michele. I also knew that the image of the tree represented her age at the time of her death, which was before she reached full maturity. As I shared this information with the recipient of the reading, she confirmed that all of the above was true. Now that is what I call a very abstract and creative way for spirit to communicate!

It always amazes me how inventive spirits are when communicating with me. They often overlap symbols, thoughts, feelings, and physical indicators to express their messages. One interesting fact, of which you may not be aware, is that our deceased loved ones in heaven also need to learn how to communicate with and through mediums. This knowledge is gained, not conferred upon us when we reside in heaven. Of course, once a soul learns how to do this, the knowledge does not go away. It grows with time and practice. I mention this because some communications involve the assistance of spirit guides, the angels, and other deceased loved ones. As a medium, I can see, sense, hear, and know when a spirit is new or inexperienced, and when they have a guide helping them to get their message through.

A Better Understanding

I hope that you now have a better understanding of how spirits communicate with mediums. I could provide numerous examples of their inventiveness and creativity; however, what I would really like you to comprehend is that the transmission of information is not as simple as having a conversation. Moreover, it is important to understand that spirits cannot be commanded by me or anyone else.

As much as you, as the recipient of a reading, may want a spirit to transmit a particular message or code that you have decided in your mind will prove that it is really them, it may be very challenging for them to do so, and they, most likely, want to spend their time sharing their message with you rather than passing a test based on your fears or disbelief. If that symbol, song title, unusual nickname, or code word is not part of my databank of memories, your loved one in spirit and I could end up wasting a lot of precious time playing a very abstract game of mediumship charades to try to translate it out. Spirits do not waste time on messages that have no meaning or are based on personal skepticism, fear, or lack of trust. They would much rather use your time, their time, and my time in a more constructive way by using identifiers that allow you to quickly validate who they are, in order to allow them the time to get their important messages through to you with clarity and love.

Misconceptions about Mediums

Contrary to popular belief, mediums are not all-knowing. We are human beings that have been blessed with divine gifts that provide us with a means of communicating with spirits. We receive the information that spirits decide they want to share with us. We do not demand or command spirits. For instance, I do not always receive proper names from spirits during a reading. Sometimes they pass that information on to me, and sometimes they do not because they send other information that clearly identifies and validates who they are to the person receiving the reading.

With my psychic and mediumship abilities, I do pick up on information in my day-to-day life and communications with others; however, I do not edge my way into people's minds or use any information I receive for harmful purposes. Everything I do is performed with love and respect; therefore, your thoughts are your personal business that I have no right or interest in reading.

The misconception surrounding the issue of being all-knowing can be amusing at times, because some people expect me to know everything there is to know about them, as well as every single one of their friends, neighbors, and deceased loved ones. When I come across someone who displays this type of behavior, I know that it is because they do not comprehend how mediumship gifts work. When it is appropriate, I kindly and briefly let them know how the gifts work and tell them that if there is something I need to know, the spiritual beings that I communicate with and my own intuition will keep me informed. Besides, knowing everything is rather boring, don't you think? What would any of us be here to learn and achieve if we already knew everything there is to know about the universe and all of its minute details? There is only one who knows all, and that is God.

On an important note, mediums should refrain from walking up to people on the street and giving readings without permission. Spirits can be very insistent when it comes to a request to share a message with someone. Before approaching anyone, a medium needs to determine whether sharing the message at that particular time is appropriate. Furthermore, the situation must be approached with respect and love for all parties involved. Instead of sharing the message right away, it may be more appropriate for a medium to introduce him or herself, let the person know that spirit has a message for them, and that they can make an appointment when they are ready to hear it. If a medium has assessed the situation and has determined that the timing and the setting is appropriate for the sharing of a message, then the medium can and should respectfully approach the person or people by introducing himself or herself, and informing the person or people that you are a medium. Kindly let the person know that a spiritual being has a message they would like you to share with them, and then ask permission to share it. If the person says "no," then respectfully thank them for their time and walk away. Spirit will know that you tried. If they say "yes," then it is acceptable to share the message as a gift to the person receiving it.

On the other side of the spectrum, if you are interested in receiving a reading by a medium, it is respectful to ask to schedule an appointment. Demanding a reading or expecting a medium to give you information or a reading just because they can, is disrespectful to spirits, the medium, and the gifts that have been bestowed upon them. I know that people are fascinated about hearing from the angels and their loved ones in heaven, and I think it is wonderful that they are genuinely interested in learning about the process; however, there is a time and a place for everything. Misinformation and misunderstanding about the gifts of mediumship run rampant in television, movies, and books. Which is why I think it is important to help people to understand that the gift of receiving a message from heaven should be approached with respect and honor.

Due to the unique nature of divine communication, it takes a lot of personal energy to provide a reading. Many mediums make their living through the utilization of their gifts, and when a person demands a reading by saying, "Oh, read me!" or asks "Who do you see around me?" or "Tell me what you see in my life?," it is the same as asking a doctor or a lawyer to give you services free of charge. They have worked hard to acquire the knowledge that they share in a professional setting, and they deserve to earn a living. The same is true for mediums who work on a professional level. Mediumship requires continual education in order to improve and refine the gifts of divine communication. Being born with the gifts is not enough, because you need to learn how to work with them. Think about this: If you met a doctor in a social setting, would you demand that he or she provide immediate non-emergency treatment or medical advice on the spot for free? If so, you may want to take a step back and think about the actions you are taking toward other people. Turn the tables and put yourself in their shoes. Would you appreciate it if someone demanded and expected you to provide a service for free when you depend upon it for income for yourself and your family? Sharing a gift of your own free will is good; however, when someone demands you to share it, it shows a lack of respect and honor for you and your profession.

Whether it is a doctor, a lawyer, or a medium, a more appropriate way to approach these situations is to ask to schedule an appointment. I do understand that people get excited about the prospect of hearing from deceased loved ones or receiving insight into their lives; however, awareness and respect for other people's professions and natural gifts goes a long way toward building positive relationships with each other.

A New Appreciation

I raise these topics to help you better understand how the gifts of mediumship work. There can be a lot of confusion or skepticism surrounding this topic. I believe it is beneficial to offer educational information to remove the veil of confusion and fear, in order to replace it with an expanded knowledge and awareness regarding the natural gifts God gives us.

Furthermore, I am greatly honored by the amazing gifts that God and the angels have bestowed upon me, and I love to share them with people who respect the blessings that such communications bring to their lives. I approach every spirit, here and in heaven, with honor, integrity, love, and respect. To share my gift with others on a full-time basis is a blessing that enables me to fulfill my life purpose to heal the spirits of those here on earth with love, which is why I call my mediumship practice *Healing Spirit with Love* (www.HealingSpiritWithLove. com). The healing of your spirit is the intention of the messages spirit in heaven shares. If truly appreciated, they can have a profoundly positive effect on your life and the way you view heaven.

Spirit communication is a wonderful and complex process that requires a tremendous amount of energy to complete. I hope that this information helps you to better understand how mediumship works and to appreciate the effort it takes from both spirit and mediums to share those incredible, blessed messages with you.

♥

Receiving Messages from Spirit through Our Senses

To communicate with those of us on earth, spirit utilizes our five main senses, our databanks of memories, and our sixth sense, which is our intuition. All of us, not just mediums, can be receivers of messages from spirit. It is a matter of being open and receptive to the messages that are being sent, as well as a well-developed intuitive sense that allows you to recognize them.

Like mediums, you may find it easier to receive messages through certain senses than through others. For example, you may be more visually oriented than feeling oriented. After you have explored your natural abilities and gifts, you can begin to work on improving your skills with all of your extrasensory senses, which are defined for you below.

Definitions and Examples of Six Metaphysical Senses

Clairvoyance—The Gift of Extrasensory Seeing

Clairvoyance is the visual receipt of information from spirit. A person with this gift is commonly referred to as a clairvoyant. Clairvoyance occurs when we see spirit fully manifested, which is sometimes referred to as a "ghost" or "entity" sighting, or in energy form, such as an orb of electric blue light. It also includes images and signs that are seen through your third eye, also referred to as your mind's eye, or recognized as an external message sent to this world by spirit. Ultimately, spirits choose the way that they would like to appear to us, as well as the messages they would like to send. When deceased human beings or pets show themselves fully manifested or through the third eye, it is usually an image or a form that represents the way they looked when they were living on earth, either toward the end of their lives, as they would best be remembered, or in the manner they would like to be remembered. When spirits send images to your third eye, they can appear as still pictures or images in motion. To give you an idea of how the third eye works, I would like to use an exercise that utilizes your ability to mentally visualize imagery. Imagine a glass of water in your mind. Place some ice cubes in the glass and some condensation beading and running down the sides. Do you see it? Do not worry if you are having a hard time seeing the glass. Not everyone can. If you can see the glass, take note of its location. As clearly as you see the glass and in the approximate location where you see it, is where you could potentially see imagery sent by spirit. When I visualize the glass, it is approximately eight to ten inches from my forehead and directly in front of me. When deceased loved ones send me images, the distance is the same; however, the images appear slightly to the right or left of center. Angels, on the other hand, appear to me in a different manner. They are very large, always in motion, and appear in a variety of forms and locations.

Visual messages from spirit can also include external signs in this world that let you know that spirit is near. Some of the more common and easy to spot include finding coins on the ground, encountering butterflies or dragonflies, and finding feathers, which are favorites of the angels. These are signs from our angels and deceased loved ones that they are around us. Other ways that spirit sends us visual signs are through numbers, images, words, or objects that remind us of deceased loved ones or the angels. It is important to note that spirits provide external visual clues that, if picked up by our intuition and recognized, can provide answers to our daily questions and guidance for living.

Clairaudience—The Gift of Extrasensory Hearing

Messages received through our sense of hearing are called clairaudient communications or clairaudience. This type of communication can be in the voice of spirit, or it can come through in your own voice in a manner similar to a thought. It can also include messages in the form of music or other sounds that have meaning for you. When you are open to and aware of the gifts that are carried within the sounds of the world, your intuition will help guide you in determining which sounds are messages from spirits. For example, I know that when I hear music playing in my mind in a seemingly random way, it is spirit sending me a message. It is my job to determine who is sending the music, as well as the message or reason for bringing that particular song to my attention by playing it in my mind. Usually, the first person I think of is the one who is sending the message. When a song by *Journey* is playing, I know it is a message from my father. He loved that band and he uses their songs to let me know he is around. He is also very clever when choosing the song because the lyrics contain his message. One of his favorites is "Don't Stop Believing." I love it when he sends me that song as a reminder to keep believing in myself and the path I am taking in my life. Thanks, Dad!

The same is true when you hear songs on the radio. Spirits have a great sense of humor, especially when it comes to messages that they send to me through music. I frequently hear music on the radio that speaks directly to a situation I am currently experiencing and, sometimes, they do it to make me laugh or to lighten up a situation. The timing of the songs is impeccable and unmistakable. I know without a doubt that it is spirit sending me a message. Has this happened to you, too? If it hasn't already, it will now, because you will be more open and aware that there are auditory messages that come to you through songs. As a note, any sound or song that you hear that is negative or contains hurtful or harmful lyrics or meanings is not spirit. Spirits would never guide you to harm yourself or others because everything they are and everything they do is based in love and respect.

Other auditory messages that you may receive include actually hearing the voice of a spirit directly in your ear or like a thought in your head that comes through in your own voice. On the biggest shopping day of the year, I woke up early to bargain-hunt with my mother.

Besides holiday presents, I was on the lookout for a new purse. I was searching for one that was either pink or purple—not my usual colors for a handbag. After looking at purses in a few stores, I was a bit discouraged because I was not finding one that fit my needs. As we were driving down the street toward our next destination, I heard the word "goodwill" in my ear, loud and clear. I laughed because I knew where they wanted me to go. I asked spirit in my mind, "You want me to stop by the Goodwill store on the biggest sale day of the year to find my purse?" The answer was, "yes." I turned to my mother and asked her if she would mind if we stopped by the Goodwill store, which happened to be on the very road we were on. She asked me why, and I told her, "Spirit wants me to go there because that is where I will find the purse that I am looking for." My mother is a believer with her own gifts, and she knows that I listen to my intuition when spirit sends me a message. Needless to say, our next stop was the Goodwill store.

As soon as I walked in, I spotted the rack of handbags at the front of the store and, lo and behold, there was a large purple purse hanging on the rack. I knew it was the one that spirit had directed me toward. The only issue was that another shopper was inspecting it at the time. I thought to myself, "Well, if this gentleman purchases it, it must mean there is another one in the store for me." With that thought in mind, I took a quick tour of the store to see if there were any other handbags that caught my eye. There were none. As I turned back to go to the front of the store, I saw that the shopper who had been looking at the purse had walked away from it, apparently deciding not to purchase it. I walked over to get a better look at this glorious purple purse. It was even better than I had imagined! It had a ton of pockets, it was very well made, and it was the perfect size. I immediately took it up to the register to purchase it. There was no price tag on it, but I did not care. I loved it, and I knew that the price would be just right. It turned out that the cost for the purse was $15.95. Wow! What a bargain! It gets even better, though. I did not realize it at the time because I was too busy loving everything else about it, but it turned out to be an authentic high-end handbag. I am not one to pay attention to name brands; however, spirit does know that I appreciate a well-made product, and this one perfectly fit my needs. Thanks, spirit! I am glad I listened to you!

The handbag story is a minor example of how, when we are tuned in to our gift of clairaudience, as well as our intuition, spirit will guide us toward objects, people, and places that help us in both small and large ways. Therefore, pay attention to the sounds you hear both internally and externally—not just music or words, but all sounds, such as bird calls, train whistles, and the like, as they may be messages from spirit sent to guide you on your soul's journey.

Clairsentience—The Gift of Extrasensory Feeling

When you feel the presence of spirit either physically or through the receipt of emotions, it is referred to as clairsentience. For example, when I give readings, I feel muted pain or heaviness in my chest when a spirit is indicating to me that they had a heart attack or a problem with their heart or lungs during the process of passing or during a significant phase of their lifetime. This information is called a validation, and it is used as an indicator to identify who it is that is coming through for you. It is important to note that as a trained medium, I am very aware of the difference between pain that is my own and a sense of pain sent by spirit. If you are experiencing unexplained pain, I would recommend that you have it checked out by a physician.

When a spirit approaches me during a reading, I usually feel their presence next to me. Males come in on the left and females on the right. There are variations as to where they place their presence that helps me to define their relationship to the person for whom I am giving a reading. The way presence of spirits is felt and how they approach can be different for each medium. For some mediums, spirits enter from one side only. As you become aware of the presence of spirits, take note of how and where you sense their form. You can also ask spirits to approach you in a certain way in order to make it easier for you to define relationships, as well as the strength of those relationships.

Beyond the sensing of a presence, spirits similarly send physical information that allows me to feel their height, their body shape, where they had distinguishing marks, mannerisms, and more. Furthermore, they send emotions through the bond that I feel as strongly as I do my own feelings. I often tell people to pay attention to my body language when I am giving a reading. That is because I may be sitting or moving in a manner that is characteristic of the spirit coming through. By asking spirits to step into my energy space or aura during a reading, I am allowing them to transmit messages to me including particular mannerisms that will help the recipient of the reading to recognize the spirit coming through. In one reading for a very good friend of mine, I was sitting at a table holding onto a coffee cup with my left hand while gently cupping the back of my neck with my right. I knew that the spirit coming through often sat this way while drinking coffee. When I brought it to the attention of the recipient, she mentioned that her deceased loved one who was coming through consistently sat in that manner. She drank a lot of coffee, and she had a problem with the back of her neck that she was constantly concerned about but was too afraid to get it checked by a doctor or specialist.

People who are strong in the gift of clairsentience are sometimes referred to as empaths or sensitives. That is because people with this gift easily pick up on the feelings and emotions of others. Clairsentients would do well to learn how to protect their personal energy space with light and love in order to prevent the unintentional picking up of others' moods and energies. One way to do this is to visualize a bright white beam of light coming down from God in heaven, entering into you through your crown chakra (located at the top of the head), traveling throughout your entire body, and continuing its journey to the core of the earth. I like to raise my arms up to the sky as I welcome the light of God, slowly lowering them to the point where they are outstretched to my right and left sides at the shoulder, and then continuing to lower them to my sides as the light travels down through my body. As the light flows through you, envision it expanding into the shape of a dome or an orb that encompasses not only your body, but also at least one arm's length beyond the reach of your outstretched arms. As you become more comfortable with this exercise, you can expand the size of the dome to two arm's lengths or even to encompass the entire universe, if you so desire. By doing so, you are expanding the protective love and the light that comes from God in order to embrace all that is within your light.

Another visualization exercise that I have used is what I call **Putting on Your Rain Slicker.** If I am entering into what I know to be a very negative environment, I envision myself with a bright yellow rain slicker on my body. It is very similar to the ones fishermen wear with an oilskin jacket, pants, and hat. Instead of repelling rain, this slicker repels negativity. When negativity heads your way, it rolls off just like rain when it hits the surface of a slicker. I think of it as added protection for those situations in which you know you will be encountering negative energies that you do not want to absorb into your spirit.

Claircognizance—The Gift of Extrasensory Knowing

Claircognizance is a little more challenging to define than the other gifts because, if you have not experienced it, it may be difficult to envision. Claircognizance is an instant sense of knowing certain information. When a download comes to you from spirit in this way, it suddenly appears in your mind, and you know without a doubt that it is true. It is different from clairaudience because with that, you hear the words and then you relay them. With claircognizance, it is as though the information descends upon my spirit and appears in my mind. Like a universal truth, I know and trust with my entire being that the information is genuine and rings true. It is an amazing and awe-inspiring experience.

At first, I mistook this gift within myself for clairaudience. I assumed that the information was coming in so fast that I was hearing and saying it at the same time. It wasn't until I stepped back and analyzed the process that I realized that I wasn't *hearing* the message, I was *knowing* it. That knowing was accompanied by a specific feeling that I define as a

133

sensing of the truth, which is tied in with my intuition or gut feelings. What helped me along the way was the recognition of a physical sign of validation that I receive from spirit. I noticed that when I was speaking information that rang true, a tingling not unlike goose bumps ran across the back of my right or left arm, across my back and up the back of my scalp, and ended on the back of the opposite arm. I continue to receive the physical signs of validation; however, I have developed my skill to the point that I readily recognize it without the added heads-up from spirit. You may have your own physical validation of a claircognizant message. My best advice is to pay close attention to the events that occur within your own body, as well as the knowing that comes along with this type of message.

Clairalience—The Gift of Extrasensory Smelling

Have you ever experienced smelling a scent, such as baking cookies or cologne, which seemed to have no explainable origin? The scent is usually strong and does not seem to fit in with what is around you. In my house, I love it when the aroma of baking cookies drifts in unexpectedly and tickles my olfactory senses. It always makes me think of my deceased Mom-Mom. And guess what? It is her stopping by to say hello and to let me know she is around.

Spirits send us messages through our sense of smell. This is called clairalient communication or clairalience. Scents are said to be some of the strongest and longest lasting of our memories. The most common ones that spirits send include colognes, perfumes, flowers scents, cigarette smoke, and various foods aromas; however, it can be any scent that you directly associate with a deceased loved one or spirit, such as the scent of the freshly turned earth or mulch that reminds you when you helped your grandfather work in the garden. Whatever scent you most strongly associate with someone is the one that they will bring through, whether it is pipe smoke, lilacs, whiskey, a mechanic's garage, or fresh paint. At first, you may turn around and look for the source of the scent. When you do not locate the source, you may dismiss it as strange and nothing else. Now that you are aware that this may be a scent sent to you by spirit, pay attention to the aroma. Who does it remind you of? If it reminds you of someone who is living, that is spirit's way of sending you a message about that person, letting you know that they are thinking of you. It may also represent a strong telepathic connection that you have with another person here on earth. When it is someone who is deceased, it is that spirit who is stopping by to say hello and to let you know that they are around. Feel free to greet them and to let them know that you love them. They hear your thoughts and love it when you acknowledge them.

Clairambience—The Gift of Extrasensory Tasting

Clairambience is the receipt of messages through the sense of taste. Clairambient messages come in the form of the actual taste of food or another substance that makes its presence known to your taste buds so strongly that it is almost as if you are ingesting it at that moment. Many times, these messages are dismissed as cravings and nothing else. Now that you are aware that cravings may sometimes be messages from spirits, you may be more inclined to determine who is sending you a message before indulging in that craving. Here is one example of how clairambient messages come through:

One day, I was standing in my kitchen when all of a sudden I could see, smell, and actually taste beef tacos. It was such a strong sense of taste that it was almost as if I was consuming them at that very moment. Of course, now that I had the taste of them in my mouth, I had a strong craving for them. Later on that evening, a very close friend of mine stopped by for a visit. We started chatting about our day, and out of the blue he mentioned that he had not eaten a lot at dinner that night because they were having tacos, which were not his favorite food. I laughed a little, and he looked at me in a slightly puzzled way. I asked him if he had sat down to dinner around five o'clock that evening. The answer was yes. I told him that it was around that time that I had tasted tacos in my mouth. We had a good laugh together about the connection we shared. This was not the first time that a clairambient experience had been shared between us.

Telepathic Connections

You may be wondering why I shared a story with you about a connection with someone here on earth. "I thought we were discussing spirit in heaven," you might say. I shared that story to demonstrate that spirit communication can occur between all of our spirits, not just with those in heaven. At our core, we are all spirit. When we are in human form, our spirits are housed within an outer shell, which is shed from our spirits when our physical bodies expire. That outer shell is what keeps us anchored to the earth. There is no difference between the spirits housed within our physical bodies and those of our heavenly counterparts, who are free of such encumbrances.

The example I gave was of a telepathic communication between spirits here on earth in the form of a clairambient message. When you are very closely connected with someone, the ability to share a connection that goes much deeper than the surface exists. It is a direct connection of spirit here on earth. People who connect deeply with plants and animals on earth experience the same type of telepathic connection, as every living thing contains energy that was created by God. We are truly connected to one another through our spirits, and we are all born with the gifts that allow us to communicate with one another in this way. It is a matter of how strong the gifts are and whether we want to develop our skills or, for some people, to even acknowledge that they exist.

Abilities and Gifts

All of us are born with the ability to communicate with spirit, whether it is in simple or complex ways. As with all gifts, some people have stronger abilities than others. For instance, the fact that I can play golf does not mean that I will win a Ladies Professional Golf Association (LPGA) tournament or even become a professional golfer, no matter how many lessons I take or how much I practice. It does mean, however, that I can enjoy the game. It is the same with psychic and mediumship gifts. Some of you may have just a touch of the gifts that allow you to utilize and enjoy them, while others of you may be or may become strong vessels for the receipt and interpretation of spirit messages. No matter what your level of ability, if spirits are meant to communicate with you, they will, whether it is directly or with the assistance of a medium whose experience with this type of communication will help you receive and interpret the messages that are meant for you.

On a side note, just because you have strong gifts of mediumship or psychic abilities, it does not necessarily mean that you are meant to become a professional medium or psychic. It could mean that you are to incorporate the use of your gifts into the work you already perform. Becoming a professional medium or psychic on a full-time basis is a calling that requires a significant amount of dedication, love, and discipline to fulfill. You will know within yourself where your path is supposed to lead. If you are still unsure, ask your angels for guidance about your life purpose, and they will certainly help you to define the path you are to take with your gifts.

Utilizing Your Intuition

One of the ways we can develop our gifts is through the use of our intuition. Each and every one of us was born with this gift. It is through our intuition that we receive messages from our higher selves, as well as the angels. These gut feelings or instincts are backed by our heavenly support teams, as well as our universal connection with one another in spirit.

There Are No Coincidences

Events that occur in your life that seem like unusual coincidences are actually the aligning of circumstances that were meant to happen. Bumping into a friend at the grocery store, finding an item you were looking for in an unexpected location, being in the right place at the right time to land your dream job, or winning the lottery just when you are in need of a windfall are all examples of events that have been orchestrated by our heavenly support teams. These events occur as answers to our prayers and requests, either as necessary steps in the evolution of our souls or the realization of our dreams. We can use our intuition, the inner voice of knowing, to decipher the signs and events that are placed before us. Or, we can choose to dismiss them with over-analyzing and logic, thereby completely missing out on the opportunities and gifts that appear as if by magic.

Invisible Assistance

The circumstances that lead to seemingly coincidental situations are orchestrated by spirits. When I say spirits, I mean God, the angels, our deceased loved ones, past spiritual masters, and spirit guides. They provide us with invisible assistance as we go throughout our days. They help us to confirm their messages through our gift of intuition. Their timing, attention to detail, and orchestration of events are an amazing phenomenon that we experience every day, whether we are aware of their assistance or not. The more aware you are of the presence of spiritual beings in your life and the way in which they operate, the more you can experience the wonder of how they play a significant role in the evolution of your life.

Miracles Happen When We Are in Sync with Heaven

Too often, we are told by naysayers that the mundane world is all there is—that the supernatural does not exist and that miracles are rare occurrences that only happen to a select few, if they happen at all. That is the chatter of the ego, the negative voice of the subconscious that blocks us from the light and from seeing the wondrous world that exists beyond the ordinary surface of our experiences. We can choose to let our egos take over and give in to the belief that what you see is what you get, or we can choose to break through the veil that covers our awareness in order to see the extraordinary that permeates our lives every day.

Seeing the Extraordinary in the Ordinary

Breaking through the veil means learning how to remove the mental barriers and blocks that have prevented us from accepting the knowledge that we truly can enjoy a connection with heaven while we are on this earth. By doing so, you can perceive life in a different and more remarkable way.

Learning how to utilize and listen to our intuition is a great place to start. There are many books and instructional guides about intuition. I recommend that you pick up the ones that resonate with you. If you are having a hard time deciding which one to read, I usually recommend *Practical Intuition* by Laura Day. When you read the book, be sure to have a digital voice recorder handy, as this will make it easier for you to perform the exercises. Laura's book helps you to recognize the signs around you and to retrain the way your mind processes the information it is receiving. I used the information in the book to learn how to see the external signs that are sent to me by my heavenly support team. Another fun way of working on your intuition is by using the book or smart phone application created by John Holland: *101 Ways to Jump-Start Your Intuition*. There are many tools and books out there that can help you to tune in to your inner voice. Please note that you are not obligated to purchase the ones I have recommended. I mention them because I have read them myself and found them useful. You may find additional resources that provide you with helpful guidance for expanding your intuitive skills. Most of all, have fun with the exploration of your gift!

The Benefits of Utilizing Your Intuition

Using your intuition to guide you will help you to look beyond the ordinary to see the extraordinary that surrounds us every day. We receive guidance on a daily basis through our intuition that provides a map directing us toward the desires we cherish most in our hearts. The more you work with your intuition, the better you will become at seeing the signs and interpreting their meanings, as well as their purpose in the overall scheme of your life.

Help Is on the Way

If you feel that you are struggling with tuning in to your intuition, feel free to ask your angels for help. They will be glad to provide you with the assistance you need. Keep an open mind and have patience. Everything will come to you at the perfect time for your development. This does not mean that it will come at the time you think is perfect, but rather at the time that they determine is perfect. Remember, the angels see and know much more than we do. Have patience, be open, and know that help is on its way.

Enjoy the Gifts You Have Been Given

Enjoy your journey, whether you are just starting out or have been tuning in to your intuition for years. An illumined mind that is attuned to the gift of intuition can reveal the threads that link your life purposes with those of others, while providing a map to guide you on your path.

Meditation Connects You to the Source and Your Soul

Meditation is essential for delving deep and tuning in to the connection that you have with yourself, as well as with all of spirit. Meditation comes in many forms. It consists of more than sitting in silence or saying "Om." In fact, sitting in absolute silence and trying to empty your mind of all extraneous thoughts is very challenging at times. I don't know about you, but trying to completely still my thoughts at times is like trying to stop a runaway train with a small pile of feather pillows.

In traditional meditation, where you sit in the silence of your soul, the breath is what is important. By concentrating on the breaths you take, you are releasing all other concerns. Once you have successfully worked on tuning out the negative thoughts that come from the ego, you will have an easier time of it because you will have learned how to handle the intrusion of thoughts that attempt to derail your peace. You will be able to recognize the thoughts for what they are and let them drift out of your mind without interrupting your meditation. In the meantime, there are easier methods of meditation that also happen to be very enjoyable.

Whenever our thoughts are not focused on the mundane issues of life, we are meditating. For instance, when you take a walk in nature and you get caught up in watching the birds or listening to the water gurgle as it rushes over rocks in a stream—you are meditating. When you are dancing to your favorite music and nothing else in the world exists except for the music, the fun, and moving your body to the beat—you are meditating. When your mind is free of its concerns or worries, it allows you to connect with your spirit, which is the purpose of meditation. Guided meditations that you can listen to live or recorded are another great way to enjoy a spiritual journey for the purpose of illuminating your soul and to connect with your heavenly support team.

Why Is Meditation Important?

The purpose of meditation is to find your center and let go of the mundane, such as the everyday worries and concerns about appointments, chores, getting the car fixed, food shopping, and money. Meditating elevates our thoughts past these inconsequential concerns to what really matters—the joy of celebrating your spirit and the love that resides within your soul. Meditation gets us back to the basics and re-attunes us to our higher selves.

The peace that we attain from meditation allows our souls to take a rest. In this time of rest, we are releasing the minute concerns about our lives that get in the way of our seeing and following our true paths. It is like cleaning debris from a road—once it is gone, you are free to proceed. In order to see the extraordinary within the ordinary in our own lives, we need to clear away the debris that collects on a daily basis. Meditation serves as one of the ways in which we can temporarily sweep aside the clutter in order to listen to our intuition.

Our Connection with God and the Angels

When our spirit is at peace within ourselves, as is the case when we are meditating, it gives us the opportunity to tune in to God and the angels. Since God resides within us, as us, when we reach within our own souls through meditation, we are reaching toward God, as well. Moreover, when we drop the intrusions of our everyday affairs, it opens the gateway for communications to and from our heavenly support teams.

Our souls cry out for peace, for answers, for guidance, and for love. We can find that by quietly going within, dismissing the thoughts of mundane concerns, and opening our hearts, minds, and spirits to God. Taking the time to meditate each day not only brings peace to our souls, but also may provide the opportunity for God and the angels to send us ideas and thoughts that may guide us toward the answers and solutions we seek.

One-on-One with God and Your Heavenly Support Team

Once you have achieved a restful state of meditation, you can reach out to God and your heavenly support team for answers to your questions. Each morning when I wake up and every evening before I go to sleep, I take the time to thank God for all that he is currently doing for me, as well as all that he has done for me. I open myself up to his love and guidance by visualizing myself cradled safely in his arms. Feelings of peace and joy wash over me as I feel God's love as it surrounds me in his embrace. I express my gratitude for his presence, assistance, and guidance, and I also take a moment to ask him questions about my life regarding particular steps I should take toward my heartfelt desires. Often, I like to use a book that has given me guidance in the past to receive his answers, such as my metaphysical books that define the meanings of crystals. While holding my book of choice, I close my eyes and say a prayer to my heavenly support team, letting them know that I come to them in the protection of the light and that I am asking for their loving guidance. I then pose my question to God or other members of my heavenly support team. With my eyes still closed, I turn to a page in the book and place my hand down onto that page. When I open my eyes, I read the passage or paragraph where my hand was placed, because that is where the answer to my question resides.

Regardless of the question you ask, it is important that you seek answers with the intention of receiving a truthful response, which means that you may receive information that is contrary to what you would like to hear. If your hand falls on a blank page, know that the answer to your question either is no or that now is not the time for the answer to be revealed to you. As a note, there are times that I have received answers that seemed to address another issue in my life instead of the one I was asking about. When this happens, it usually means the issue that was addressed has more significance than the one I was asking about.

This practice of asking for and receiving answers from God and my heavenly support team is something that I have been successfully utilizing for almost twenty years. The original idea for it came from *The Enchanted Tarot* by Amy Zerner and Monte Farber. Over the years, I have expanded the scope of the practice and uncovered additional insight into the way that spirit responds to requests for information. I pass it on to you today as a gift that may provide you with the answers you seek while strengthening your relationship with your heavenly support team.

As you complete your meditations or sessions with God and your heavenly support team, send them a message of gratitude through your thoughts for their love and guidance. They love to know that you appreciate their efforts on your behalf.

Deciphering the Messages within Your Dreams

There are many theories about what dreams really are, such as random images brought forth from the subconscious, meaningful messages from our higher selves, or a means for the subconscious to process the events of our lives as we sleep. To me, dreams are an interesting phenomenon brought forth from our higher selves, as well as from our heavenly support teams of deceased loved ones, the angels, God, past spiritual masters, and spirit guides. Dreams utilize the copious images, feelings, and thoughts within our databanks of memories to create story lines that are played out while we sleep. These visions can be interpreted with an open mind and lots of practice, practice, practice.

How to Remember Your Dreams

Some of you may be thinking, "But I don't dream." Science has proven that we all dream several times per sleep session during the rapid eye movement (REM) cycle.[3] It is called that because our eyes frequently shift back and forth beneath our closed eyelids as we travel through our dreams.

The reason we have a difficult time remembering our dreams may have to do with when we wake up during our sleep cycles. There is a method I employ that helps me to wake up at the appropriate time. I have found that if I make a conscious effort to remember my dreams, I do remember at least one upon waking. It works by using my mind to alert my body to wake up during the REM cycle. Before I go to sleep, I tell myself that I would like to remember my dreams upon waking. Do not worry if this does not happen right away for you. Keep trying because success will come in time. You can also ask your angels for help. They would be glad to assist you not only with your internal wake-up call, but also with the interpretation of the dreams you remember upon awakening.

Recording Your Dreams

There are many books on the market about dream interpretation, such as dream dictionaries, that try to help you to determine what your dreams are about. Unfortunately, the definitions for the symbols and objects within the dream dictionaries may not ring true for you, because the symbols and objects may have different meanings for you than they do for someone else. The dictionaries may help you with basic universal symbols that are common to your cultural background; however, your own databank of

---

3   See http://science.howstuffworks.com/life/what-are-dreams.htm for the scientific explanation of dreams and sleep cycles.

memories provides the best basis for interpreting the symbols, objects, and events that come forth in your dreams. For instance, there is a woman I know who adores snakes. To her, the appearance of a snake in her dreams would most likely be a positive symbol because of the relationship she has developed with them. For others, snakes can be a negative symbol or a source of fear and nightmares due to the lack of understanding about the nature of snakes or the way they have been culturally portrayed. Because many people have a fear of snakes, the dream dictionaries may indicate that the appearance of one in your dreams is a symbol of your fears. As pointed out by the example above, this may not be the case for you. The most effective way to interpret your dreams is to do it yourself, because only you know what your symbols mean to you.

Prepare the Night Before

In preparation for dream remembrance, I keep a notebook and a pen, my iPad, or a voice recorder by my bedside. Having a readily available source for recording your dreams is important. Once you get up and start your day, the details of your dream may begin to fade fast. If you record your dream as soon as you wake up, before you even get out of bed, you will be able to capture more detail.

When recording your dream, especially when you are writing it down, do not worry about grammar, spelling, or order; just write down everything you can recall as quickly as possible. Think of it as a stream of consciousness style of writing in which you record everything that is flowing through your mind without concerning yourself about proper sentence structure. Write your dream down or record it in the order in which you remember it, with as much detail as possible. After you have completed the capturing of your dream sequences, you can always add notes if you need to reorder the sequences or add a detail here and there.

The next action you take is to set aside what you just wrote or recorded. **Do not try to interpret your dream right away.** Forget all about your dream and what you wrote or recorded for at least a few hours or a day. When you are ready to pick it up again for interpretation, it is important for you to have an open mind because you are going to use word association to decipher your message. If you dictated your dream into a voice recorder, transcribe it into written form right away or right before you are ready to decipher it.

Using Word Association to Define the Symbols, Objects, and Events

Are you ready to interpret your dream? If so, grab a pen and paper. Look at the symbols and objects in your dream. Take it one section at a time. For instance, let us imagine that in your dream you are driving a car down a large four-lane highway. Without thinking about it too much, write down the first thing you think of when you think of a car. For me, I think of a mode of transportation or something that gets me from one location to another. What comes to mind when you think of a large four-lane highway? I think of an open road or a long-distance road trip. For you, a car or the highway may mean something completely different. There is no right or wrong answer. Just remember to use the word association exercise and try not to think too much about your answer. Whatever you think of first is what that symbol or object means to you.

Important note: If you pause or think too much about a symbol, you may distort the meaning. Do not attempt to force a meaning to a symbol or attempt to decipher the overall message of your dream just yet. Concentrate on the symbols, objects, and events as isolated items that are not related to one another.

Repeat the word association exercise for all of the objects within your dream, as well as all of the actions. For instance, were you driving toward a particular destination or person? Away from somewhere, someone, or something? Joy riding? Were you being chased? Was anyone in the car with you? Were there other vehicles on the road? All of these factors are important.

Emerging Themes

After you have provided the associated words for all of the symbols, objects, and events, go back and see if there is a theme that is emerging from the words you wrote down. Keep an open mind. You should see a theme emerging that correlates to a situation that is currently occurring in your life. For instance, with the car dream, I may have a strong desire to free myself from responsibilities and obligations in order to travel on a new path—to hit the open road and experience a feeling of being free and looking forward to new adventures. You may not be able to see the theme or themes right away. Look to see if there is a connection between the associated words that you wrote. How do they tie in with the actions taking place in your dream? What events are occurring in your life? What topics are you struggling with? Your dreams may be providing you with clues as to what is at the heart of the topics and events that are causing you concern or worry in the waking world.

Your dream may be a reflection of your subconscious trying to work through the details of your hopes and concerns. It does not mean that the situation will turn out the way your dream did. Remember, it is a message that is delivered in many shades of gray that require interpretation. Just because you see yourself dying in a dream, it does not mean that you are going to die. Dreams are not that literal. A dream about dying may have to do with your need to overcome your fear of death. Your heavenly support team may be sending you a message that your fear of dying is interfering with the living of your life. Moreover, they may be trying to help you to release that fear by showing you images of heaven or by dropping into the dream itself in spirit.

Visits from Deceased Loved Ones in Your Dreams

Whenever you see your deceased loved ones in your dreams, it really is them. They like to assist you in both your waking and sleeping hours. Dreams give them the opportunity to let you know they are around because your daytime defenses are down. When you encounter a deceased loved one in your dreams, feel free to say hello. Just know, though, that you might wake yourself up in the process because you are interrupting the natural dream sequence. I did that many times when I saw my father in my dreams and had to laugh at myself when I accidentally woke myself up. As with anything else, practice makes perfect. Dreams are tricky; too much interruption in the message, and you wake yourself up.

I would also like to note that I have come across many people who are disappointed that they have not seen a particular deceased loved one in their dreams. My next question to them is: "Where are you in the grief process? Have you fully accepted and come to terms with this particular person's passing?" Often, I find that people who have not encountered a particular loved one in their dreams have not truly accepted the ending of this person's life on earth or, more importantly, that this person's spirit continues to live on beyond its earthly existence. Your deceased loved ones are not punishing you by not showing up in your dreams; rather, they are patiently waiting for you to work through the process of grieving in order to arrive at a place of acceptance and understanding regarding the natural cycles of endings and new beginnings that occur for all spirit.

Practice and Epiphanies

With regard to interpreting your dreams, it is important to adopt a relaxed and stress-free attitude about the process. In the beginning, you may have a little trouble seeing the themes or working with word association. Relax. It will come to you with practice. You may even experience unexpected epiphanies later in the day that reveal the true meaning of your dream to you. I have experienced this many times. If the themes are not emerging for me right away, I set my dream and the notes about my dream aside, and continue on with other activities. Then, without even trying, a complete understanding of my dream and its message washes over me. It is as if my mind was working on it in the background and has suddenly deciphered the meaning for me. It is a mind-blowing experience when it happens, as the sudden and complete understanding comes as a wonderful surprise and gift that can literally stop you in your tracks. I love it when epiphanies like this happen in my life not only about dreams, but also about topics or issues I have been trying to make sense of in my mind.

Most of all, I hope you enjoy your journey into the world of your dreams. The messages are there for you, and you can interpret them with an open mind, practice, and assistance from your heavenly support team.

The Beauty and Messages in Music

Music is a fantastic auditory experience that speaks to our spirits and deeply affects us. Whether we are conscious of it or not, sounds and music are around us at all times. The original music of the earth was composed by the sounds of nature—the leaves rustling in the trees, the birds singing their melodies, rain dancing as it meets the ground, the deep bass of the rumbling earth as it formed, and the hushed mingling of the snow as frozen flakes gently settle upon one another. Those sounds and their music are still with us today as the underlying basis of all music.

Human Contributions Guided by Heaven

Human beings have greatly contributed to the growth of music through the creation of sounds of their own and, over time, have developed more and more complex rhythms, melodies, and combinations of auditory notes. When we hear music, it is not a jumble of sounds mashed together, but an incredible blending of sounds designed to reach out and touch our souls. Music is a powerful emotional stimulator that has a very unique effect on our lives. It can make us laugh, cry, or want to dance. Moviemakers use it all of the time to stir our emotions while we are watching their films.

What is interesting about music is that much of it comes from heaven. From our heavenly paradise, spirits work with musicians as invisible muses, inspiring and sharing musical scores and lyrics with artists to send messages to individuals, as well as the world. All music, whether it is joyful or sad, carries within it a story that is received through our auditory senses and deciphered by our minds.

Messages Intended for Us

Every day, we hear songs on the radio, jingles on television, soundtracks from movies, streaming on the Internet, someone singing a song as they walk down the street, and music in our minds. The songs may seem random; however, at times, they carry messages of import from your heavenly support team.

Did you ever have a song come on the radio that matched exactly what you were thinking at that very moment or expressed exactly how you felt about a particular situation in your life? This is spirit's way of sending you messages. Whether it is the answer to a question or an empathetic response to your current plight, spirits let you know that they are there for you. By listening and becoming aware of the sounds and music that surround you, you can benefit from the messages that they are sending to you.

Paying Attention to What We Hear

When you have a song playing in your head, have you ever wondered why you are hearing it? I am talking about the random songs that seem to pop into your head for no reason that you can fathom. Take a moment to listen to the song that is playing in your mind. What is the title? What are the lyrics? Who or what does it make you think of? The song, as well as the lyrics, may be providing you with an answer to a problem that you are experiencing, or it may be a deceased loved one who is letting you know they are near.

The messages can be somewhat abstract in nature. Because of that, it may take a little practice to interpret them. Over time, you will become better at deciphering the messages spirits are sending you. Be sure to listen to your intuition, as it will be the best guide and source of confirmation for what you are hearing. For instance, the song you are hearing may bring up memories of a particular time of year, which may be your answer as to when an event will occur or your problem will be resolved. On the other hand, it may be providing you with an actual answer to a problem you are facing. The key is to be aware of what was on your mind the moment the song started to play in your head. The message you are receiving may be an answer to the situation you were pondering.

Messages from Deceased Loved Ones

Songs may also turn your thoughts toward memories of a deceased loved one. This is a message from your deceased loved one that they are with you and supporting you with their love. For me, when I hear the song "Michelle" by *The Beatles* in my head, I know that my best friend, Michele, who passed away more than two decades ago, is nearby and sending me her love. At other times, when I was struggling with a particularly vexing issue, I would hear "All You Need Is Love." That *Beatles* song is a lovely reminder sent to me by my heavenly support team that always makes me smile and helps me to get back to what really matters, the giving and receiving of love.

Negative Music Is Not a Sign from Spirit

It is important to note that music that carries hateful or violent messages is not a sign or message from spirits, but a reflection of souls who have not yet seen the light. The deep angst and anger that causes musicians to compose that kind of music represents the darkness that could take over our lives if we do not strive to overcome the negative messages of ego that are based on the illusion of fear.

Enjoy the Messages in the Music

By becoming more aware of your personal soundtrack of music—that which you hear in your mind or that drifts into your ears at just the right time—will enable you to better recognize the auditory messages and signs from spirits that you have been receiving all along. The messages and signs are there—all you need to do is listen.

Enjoy the music and the messages!

Sharing
the Love

There Are Two Motivating Factors: Love and Fear

In learning how to get along with other human beings on earth, it is important to understand what motivates both you and other people. We are given two choices. We can take action based on the precepts of love, or we can take action based on the precepts of fear.

What Is Fear?

Fear is an illusion. It is a mechanism of the ego that was designed as an obstacle to be overcome while living our lives on this earth. It is the reason negativity exists. When we listen to the voice of ego, which is filled with fear, we are driven off the path of our life purposes and soul evolvement.

Fear is a learned response. In our formative years, we watch and learn from the people and beings around us. It is during this time of exploration that we are learning about what is right and wrong. We are taught to fear certain situations because we do not like the

163

consequences. It can be an instinctual response, such as when you pull your hand back from a fire. The pain you feel from the heat sends a signal to your brain to remove your hand from the heat because it hurts. A fear of fire can then develop which, under extreme conditions, may lead to a strong aversion to fire. On the other hand, a healthy respect for fire can also develop, which allows for the proper use of fire with recognition for its properties and benefits.

People react with fear for many reasons; however, most of the time, it stems from past experiences that caused physical or emotional pain. Fear can be an emotional red flag signaling that there is a situation from the past that still requires processing. If we can get to the root of our fears, we can release them, recognize the lessons that were to be learned, and be grateful for the experience. If left unaddressed, fears can take over our lives. For example, a fear of the unknown could be based on an unexpected situation that had negative connotations from the past. Due to this experience, a person might then choose to be afraid of all situations in which they feel they do not know what the outcome will be. This can emotionally paralyze a person to the point that they take few or no risks in life and, as a consequence, miss out on numerous opportunities to be happy and realize their dreams.

It is very important to note that our reactions are our choice. We decide how we react to each situation we encounter in our lives. This includes how we react to the way other people treat us and speak to us.

What Is Love?

Love is the strongest, most powerful, and most enduring energy in the universe. It endures and lives within our spirits for as long as our spirits are in existence. It is the driving motivation of God, which, in turn, is the driving motivation of us. We can choose to ignore it or embrace it. That is the beauty of the gift of free will. It is one of the reasons we were put on this earth—to decide whether to live in the reality of love or in the illusion of fear.

How Can We Live in Love and Not Get Caught Up in Fear?

The answer is as simple as making a choice for each and every situation you encounter. It may be challenging to overcome the negative programming of your past, but it is not impossible. It does take work and a conscious effort. Your first reaction to a situation may be based on fear, but if you take a step back and recognize what is going on, you can learn to see life from a different perspective.

Looking at the Motivational Factors of a Situation

I was recently confronted by a situation with a friend of mine who, instead of sharing my joy about a positive development in my life, he decided to react with a sarcastic comment about how "great" it was and vehemently continued the diatribe with: "Why do good things always seem to happen for you and not me?" Needless to say, I was initially disappointed in this reaction, as I had hoped my friend would be truly happy for me. Instead of sharing in my happiness, my friend decided to react with jealousy and self-pity. I could have allowed my friend's negative mood and reaction to bring me down; however, I chose instead to look at the situation from a perspective of love.

My friend's reaction was based on the fear that positive events would not happen to him—that they only occur for other people. It is interesting to note that this particular friend is in the habit of blocking opportunities with a defeatist attitude based on a fear of failure or even of success. This person is afraid of taking risks and, because of that, he refuses to take a chance on achieving his dreams. Instead, he denies himself the opportunity for happiness before the opportunity has a chance to develop. In recognizing that my friend's negativity was based upon his own fears, I was able to let go of my disappointment in my friend's reaction and move on with my life. I did try to talk to my friend about his ability to make his dreams come true; however, I know that it is entirely up to him to see the truth of the situation. When he recognizes the problem he created and takes responsibility for blocking positive experiences, he will then be able to move past the self-imposed obstacles to his personal happiness.

There are some people you encounter that have no desire to improve or change their lives, even though they complain about their lives as often as they can. People who play the role of the martyr often bemoan that nothing works out well in their lives, that everyone is against them, and that they cannot seem to do anything right. In reality, it is their own fears and lack of belief in themselves that blocks their progress and happiness. This may be due to a strong lack of self-esteem that stems from past experiences. Often this is compounded by the decision to give away their power to someone else by accepting harsh words and treatment as a judgment of their personal character. What a person in this situation may not understand is that when someone treats us badly, it is not a reflection of who we are, but a reflection of the fears within the person inflicting the harm. We choose how we react to those words and actions. We can either let the people attempting to hurt us to damage our beliefs about ourselves, or we can look beyond the surface and see that this person is projecting their own fears upon us, which we do not have to accept or tolerate.

Unproductive Emotions

Hatred and jealousy are unproductive and hurtful emotions that harm you, not the person toward which those negative feelings are directed. We are all here following our own paths, and we are all learning lessons at different times. Harboring pessimistic or bitter feelings within yourself about your own progress and projecting it toward others is an example of living in fear. When someone has a relationship, success, or objects that you do not possess at the moment, it is not a sign that you are a failure or that you are doomed to never attaining those things for yourself. Rather, it is a sign that the person who is experiencing positive events is on the right path and has received an answer to a prayer. This is an experience that should be celebrated in the spirit of love and support. It can also be viewed as a hopeful sign that good events are possible in all of our lives. Remember, when it comes to your own life, you make choices every day about the path you will take. If your thought processes are based in fear, you will draw toward you the very situations you are envisioning, which is most likely what you do not desire. If your thought processes are based in love, you will draw toward you what you truly desire in your heart. Being envious of others robs you of opportunities for happiness and success because you are too busy being concerned about them and not about you.

When I encounter people who express negativity toward me that is not legitimate feedback about my own behavior upon which I could improve, I choose not to take it personally or let it bother me. In my mind, I wish the person well and ask the angels to help this particular person remove the veil of fear that is preventing them from experiencing the love that is within their own heart. Most importantly, I do not take their criticism to heart because I know that the words that they speak are coming from a lack of understanding regarding the negative emotions and situations that they have yet to process in their own lives.

Healing Is Possible

There is a lot of healing that could take place for people who internalize the harsh messages and treatment from others, or who allow fear to rule their lives. In order for this to happen, the person who is giving their power away to others must come to realize that they are responsible for their fate. Believing in oneself and learning how to assertively speak up for oneself is a great way to begin the healing process. In addition, forgiveness for past mistakes on the part of the people who hurt them, as well as for the mistakes that they themselves have made, is integral for releasing detrimental feelings that have built up over time. It takes a lot of diligence and hard work to overcome a lifetime of harmful habits that keep us from achieving our dreams. However, if you make a commitment to yourself and stick by it, you will succeed. Know, too, that professional counseling can be a wonderful way to work through the issues that have been holding you back. Sometimes, it is very helpful and appropriate to speak to an unrelated third party who is trained in psychology or psychiatry with whom you can objectively discuss the issues you are facing in your life. They can help you to uncover the reasons for the problems you face, as well as teach you how to better cope with the challenging situations that you may encounter on a day-to-day basis.

Managing the Ego

I readily admit that the negative voice of the ego still edges its way into my life. With practice, I have learned how to temporarily shut down the voice of ego; however, it is an on-going process. The ego is a part of my being here on earth, and it is persistent in its efforts to drag fear into the happiest of moments. It does get easier, though, to manage that nagging voice of illusion. That said, there is no reason to feel bad about yourself if your fears get the best of you from time to time. Extend compassion toward yourself, as well as toward others. We are all human beings on a spiritual journey. We all slip up and make mistakes every now and then. What is important is how we react to those mistakes, whether we extend forgiveness toward ourselves and others, what we learn, and how we conduct ourselves from that point forward.

Opening Up to Understanding

In recognizing the motivational factors that influence our lives and the lives of others, we can become much more understanding and compassionate toward ourselves and one another. In this way, we are opening up our lives to allow love to rule the day, not fear.

The most toxic energy is fear, because it can lead to hatred, intolerance, and violence, which are all more lethal than any substance we can put in our bodies or any disease. A more positive way of gaining understanding about other people and situations is to educate yourself and to recognize that each of us is doing the best we can with what we have. We are all on different levels of evolvement, and it is important to remember that we made conscious choices to come back to this earth to learn soul lessons, as well as to help one another as we travel on our purposeful life paths. Kindness and compassion go a long way toward making our pathways easier to follow, as well as much more enjoyable.

Reasons for Being

There is a reason why certain people enter into our lives. Often, these people have agreed to assist us with the lessons we chose to learn in order for our souls to evolve during our time on earth. We choose the specific lessons that we will learn before we are born into this world; however, the ways in which situations will come about are yet to be determined. For instance, we may choose to learn how to overcome devastating personal pain in order to see the blessings in the situations we encounter in life. On earth, that lesson may come to us in the form of verbal and physical abuse by a close relative, friend, or significant other that gives us a choice to either succumb to feelings of a lack of self-worth and little to no self-confidence, or to rise up to feelings of accomplishment for removing ourselves from the situation and recognizing the opportunity it offered us to appreciate our inner strength and love for ourselves. It may have also enabled us to be more empathetic and understanding toward others who have lived through similar situations. Often, there are multiple lessons rolled into one situation that have the potential to benefit you, as well as all of the people involved. The value we receive from the circumstances we encounter lies in the choices we make and whether we recognize the lessons and blessings.

Soul Groups and Soul Contracts

In the process of making decisions about your soul's evolvement, members of your soul groups volunteer to help with certain lessons, and you volunteer to help with theirs. These agreements are referred to as soul contracts. They are stored within the *hall of records*, which is maintained by the angels in heaven.

Specific people enter our lives to help us fulfill our soul contracts or to assist us with steps we need to take toward the realization of our life purposes. Either way, these people are there for a significant reason. For instance, a member of your immediate soul group may volunteer, during the process of creating soul contracts in heaven, to pass away on earth at the age of twenty-seven. This may be done in order to help you and other members of your soul group to learn how to cope with tragedy, as well as to understand that death is not the end of the spirit. The love that connects us never dies, as long as our spirits are in existence. Others may help us to learn to overcome the fear that holds us back from realizing our dreams.

Most soul contracts involve a complex set of lessons that serve multiple purposes for multiple people. When we are born on earth, the knowledge and awareness that we had about the contracts we made in heaven is obscured from us. This is because part of our journey as souls is to rediscover the reasons we are here. The more we seek out the depth and breadth of this knowledge, the more in tune we are with our life purposes, which enables us to more readily see the lessons that we are learning and sharing.

The Choice Is Ours

Free will always plays a role in whether the lessons you have chosen to learn will be completed. That is why the manner in which lessons come into your life is left to be decided by your choices on earth. If you choose not to learn a particular lesson, whether consciously or subconsciously, it will come back to you repeatedly in this lifetime. For instance, if fear is blocking you from manifesting your dreams, situations will come up that will help to teach you about overcoming your fears. These situations may include conversations with others, books or articles you read, new people you meet, and circumstances that demonstrate the positive impact of courage backed by love.

It is important to note that the angels and God are continuously giving you the tools you need to succeed with your soul's evolvement. It is your choice whether you do or do not listen to the guidance you are freely given from heaven.

With regard to your life lessons, the time will come for you to put what you have learned into action. If you succeed, you will move on to the next lesson. If you do not, you will be prevented from moving forward in your life until you have learned all of the lessons connected with this particular situation.

You may know someone—or you may even be someone—whose life lessons have ground to a halt. A person in this situation seems to struggle and be stuck in a pattern, whether it is harmful relationships, addictions, negative thinking, or self-inflicted emotional pain. This person is struggling within themselves and is having a hard time overcoming a particular lesson. People who are in this situation require compassion, even if it is challenging to give it to them. They should not be looked down upon just because they have not learned a specific lesson. Instead, send them love and kindness in prayer, ask the angels to help them, and assist them yourself if you can. Please know, though, that the decision to move forward is ultimately up to them. You cannot make their choices for them because you do not control them, just as they do not control you. It is important to recognize when a situation becomes too painful and draining for you. You do not have to stay in a relationship or situation that is causing you more pain than good, such as when you are being subjected to physical or emotional abuse, or when the person involved is constantly taking from you, essentially making you their crutch. In these instances, feeding the negative situation only encourages more of the same behavior. Professional help may be required to heal both you and the person who is wrapped up in the negative patterns they have embraced. It is better to recognize the need for professional intervention and to remove yourself from a harmful situation than to allow it to drown you with its sorrow. It may be challenging to do; however, it is vital that you respect yourself enough to know when a situation is toxic and beyond your abilities to repair. Ask God to help you release the situation from your life, pray for the health and happiness of those involved, and take steps to move forward into healthier relationships.

Taking Responsibility

The bottom line is that we are all responsible for our own growth and the direction that our lives will take. We are here not only to move forward with the evolution of our souls, but also to provide support for others with compassion and understanding based on a perspective of love. At times, that love requires us to make tough choices that appear to counter the love in our hearts for others. In actuality, it is the love that you have for others, as well as for yourself, that enables you to make the decisions that will ultimately benefit all parties involved.

♥

Unity, Peace, and Love

Soul contracts can be formulated within our immediate soul groups, such as our families and friends, as well as with larger soul groups of which we are a part. These soul groups can include our hometowns, states, provinces, or countries. The largest soul group includes all of spirit as a whole.

When a soul contract is made that affects a considerable amount of people, it is designed to create an important impact on the mindset of the group. These may include either positive events, such as the election of a dedicated and benevolent leader, or negative events, such as a war between countries.

Discovering Unity amidst Disaster

Significant tragic events that affect an entire community or country, including natural disasters or an unexpected attack on the safety of citizens, can have a unique effect on the thinking patterns of those affected. It is extremely unfortunate that these adverse events occur; however, instead of dragging people down, they can sometimes serve as crucial reminders that we are here on this earth to support and love one another. Please know, though, that it is not necessary for these events to occur in order for us to embrace the unity of our spirits.

In the aftermath of a large-scale tragic event, it is amazing and wonderful to see large groups of people working as one in the face of calamitous events that threaten to wreak havoc on a community or that attempt to devastate a country and its people. When we band together like that, it is as if we are all reminded that we are angels on earth, standing shoulder-to-shoulder and helping each other physically, mentally, emotionally, and spiritually. Old hurts and past grudges are forgotten as the priorities and basic necessities of the moment are assessed and addressed. People draw together and lend a hand to help those in need and to do what they can to restore order and calm. Physical aid and emotional comfort are extended to those who need it, and prayers for healing flood heaven's inboxes.

When Push Comes to Shove

As with almost any situation that requires a definitive decision, when push really comes to shove, fear takes a backseat and love takes over. The ego, with its petty whining and "I can't do this" attitude, is silenced, because we do not have time for nonsense and the illusion of fear. It is at this time that people discover that they have rich, untapped potential within themselves. They take actions they never thought they could, including rushing into the face of danger to save the life of a fellow human being or an animal.

These negative situations are sometimes meant to be wake-up calls for large groups of people who have become mired in fear-driven ideology. As contradictory as it sounds, a soul contract such as this was designed to positively impact as many people as possible. Good can always be found in negative circumstances because they are often a catalyst for the growth of our souls. For people who are already in a positive mindset, the event is a confirmation of what they already knew—that we can accomplish great feats when we move past our fears and honor the connection in spirit that we have with every being in the universe.

Striving for Unity and Peace

Each and every day, we can continually strive to live in unity and peace with one another by sharing the love and compassion within our hearts. The more we do this, the better the world will be for all of us. There will still be those that turn to violence and fear, but if we counter their negative actions with the connective love that unites our spirits, then the effects of tragic events will cease to hold us in a destructive pattern. Striving for unity and peace has the potential to noticeably decrease the opportunity for these events to occur.

My prayer today, and every day, is for all of us to live in love and to help each other experience the light within each and every one of our hearts and souls. With honor, respect, and love, we can move forward together to make this world a better place.

♥

How We Can Be Angels on Earth

As we greet each day, we have hopes and dreams that we would like to see fulfilled—whether it is for a new job, for a loved one to get well, or to find people with whom we can develop positive relationships. In each of our hearts, we hold our individual dreams that we would love to see realized in a way that would benefit not only us, but also our loved ones.

As spiritual beings on a human journey, we are here to help each other bring those life-affirming dreams to fruition. We have been tasked with the job of being angels on earth by assisting and supporting one another during times of need, as well as during times of joy and celebration.

Helping to Answer Prayers

On some occasions, without our even knowing it, we may be called upon by God or the angels to answer the prayers of others. For instance, your interactions with others may provide answers to problems you did not know they had, or your random acts of kindness may bring happiness to a heart that has been riddled with sadness and grief.

On other occasions, you may make conscious choices to help those in need, such as coming to the aid of someone who has been injured in a car accident. In my work as a spirit medium, I have made the decision to dedicate myself to the healing of spirit here on earth as a vessel through which spirit in heaven communicates. Others of you may have chosen to be a caregiver, an environmentalist, a teacher, a veterinarian's assistant, or a people manager. No matter what your vocation, you can contribute to the well-being of others in your own unique ways. For example, you can choose to volunteer your time or resources to people or animals who need you. This may take the form of donating gently used clothing and items, lending a hand to a friend, giving a gift of time or money to charity, adopting a pet, or caring for children and taking an interest in their upbringing.

Ways You Can Be an Angel on Earth

There are numerous ways for us to contribute to the positive energy of this world. The best way to do it is to share the talents and abilities that you enjoy, because that will multiply the positive effects for everyone involved. Beyond the mediumship services that I provide through my *Healing Spirit with Love* practice, I love to volunteer my time and skills to local charities and friends by cooking delicious meals, sorting and packaging toys for children, and caring for animals. It is very rewarding to see the results of my labors directly affecting the people and animals in my local communities. This includes the recipients of the assistance, as well as the people who are running the charities. The people in charge of organizing and disseminating charitable donations and support have made it their mission to help others. By lending them assistance, we become an important part of the cycle of giving, because without our time, money, and skills, the recipients of the charity's largesse may not receive the help they need to overcome illness, to clothe their families, or to eat nutritious and balanced meals.

Love's Return on Investment

I believe in the expression: "What goes around, comes around." I know that as I am helping people, others are helping me. The same happens for you. Your investment of love in the spirit and well-being of others will be returned to you in ways that will bring you contentment and joy. God and the angels appreciate it when you apply a helping hand to their work by being an angel on earth. When your prayers are answered and your dreams come true, be sure to share your appreciation and gratitude to the universe for the gifts you have been given, both big and small. By doing so, you are recognizing the efforts and sacrifices others have willingly made on your behalf.

Each day, I give gratitude to God and the angels for granting me the time and resources to share the love in my heart with all of us in spirit here on earth and in heaven. It is my hope and my prayer that you, too, have many reasons to give and receive gratitude every day as you fulfill your life purpose as an angel on earth.

♥

Bringing Out the Best
in Yourself and Others

It is amazing to see someone living up to his or her potential. In order for this to happen, a person needs to have inner strength, courage, and faith, as well as encouragement and support. God and the angels continuously surround us with their love and lend us their strength as we face obstacles and achieve triumphs. As partners in spirit on a human journey, we can supplement their support by extending compassion, love, and respect toward one another, as well as toward ourselves. One of the ways that we can bring out the best in ourselves and others is by relating to one another on a heartfelt level through honest communications.

We Are All Interesting Spirits

People are fascinating. I love learning about each individual I meet because each person has such interesting and incredible stories, as well as talents and abilities, which bring wonder and light to this world. What I find, though, is that sometimes people get so wrapped up in negativity and everyday concerns that they forget all of those wonderful qualities they have, and they forget to take the time to enjoy the activities that make their souls sing. Genuine communication is the key that unlocks the door to our hearts, as it allows both your light and the light of the person with whom you are conversing to shine.

Be Yourself

When interacting with someone, whether it is the cashier at the convenience store or your best friend, the more genuine you are with yourself, the more genuine you are with others. It does not matter if it is a one-minute or one-hour conversation; just be yourself, and your own light will already be shining. When this happens, there is an ease of knowing who you are that allows you to speak with others from the heart. It is amazing to see how people glow and open up when you speak from your heart to theirs—you can actually see how their light shines brighter around them.

Speak from the Heart

Heartfelt communication is about empathy, relating, and respect, as well as honesty, listening, sharing, and responding. Understanding and compassion come through when you take the time to truly acknowledge a fellow soul. It is the kindness that you bestow upon others in your interactions that uplifts their souls, as well as your own.

For people who are shy or who have a hard time starting a conversation, do not worry. A genuine smile shared while meeting someone's eyes with your own can also be a great way to share positive interactions with others. If you are interested in learning how to talk to people and would like to know how to start a conversation, here are some tips:

- ♥ Ask someone how they are doing and mean it. Listen to their answer, even if they give you an automatic "Fine, thanks" in response. If they respond with a more in-depth answer, pick up on what they are talking about and ask another question regarding the topic. For instance, if someone states that they are a little tired or excited, ask why with sincerity. They will tell you their story.

- ♥ When people ask how you are doing, be heartfelt with your answer and expand it beyond the habitual response of "Fine, thanks."

- ♥ Take note of your surroundings. Think about the person with whom you are speaking and the kinds of questions you can ask them to open a conversation. You can start with something as safe as the weather; however, as you become more confident, learn to look for a topic that is more interesting to talk about. As an example, on a cruise ship when you are seated at a table for dinner with people you just met, you can ask them all kinds of questions about why they chose that particular cruise and destination, what shore excursions they are participating in, what they like best about the ship, what they enjoy most about cruising, whether this is their first cruise, and so on.

♥ Be sure to allow the other person a chance to ask you questions, as well. A back-and-forth exchange opens the communication up to a conversation instead of what could be perceived as an interrogation or interview session. Answer genuinely and with honesty.

♥ Truly listen when others are speaking.

♥ Respect your boundaries and theirs. If you are uncomfortable talking about a certain topic, politely let the person know that you do not wish to discuss it. If someone tells you that he or she is not comfortable sharing certain information, respect his or her wishes and change the topic of conversation to a less controversial subject.

♥ Smile and make eye contact as you speak and as you actively listen to the responses you are given.

Try Not to Take a Bad Mood Out on Others

If you are having a bad day and your mood is really sour, try to take a moment before you spread that negativity to the next person you meet. Acknowledge to yourself that you are having a rough time and let go of the angst. Ask the angels to help you to elevate your mood and to release the negative thoughts and emotions you are experiencing. Try to go and do something positive for yourself, even if it is only a short walk; taking deep, relaxing breaths to find your center; or listening to a favorite piece of music that uplifts your mood. If you need to talk to a friend to help you work through the issues, do just that. As for the many people you come into contact with throughout your day, do your best to consciously decide not to pass on that black cloud to someone else. Again, if you need help getting through a rough patch, ask for help from your angels, as well as your friends and family. That is one of the reasons they are in your life—to help you work through the many complex issues and lessons we learn as our souls evolve.

Genuine Communication Is Good for the Soul

The next time you meet someone, speak from the heart. Think about what it is like to be them and what it would mean to you if someone was genuinely interested in what you had to say. You will be amazed at how easy it is to connect with other souls on a sincere level and how good it feels to be yourself. The person you communicate with benefits as well, because you are giving them a gift from the heart, which would brighten anyone's day.

The Wonders
of Nature

♥

Our Spiritual Relationship
with Animals

Just as our human bodies house a beautiful spirit, our animal friends also shine with the light of their own spirits. People with pets know that the animals in their lives have unique personalities and attributes that are very similar to those of humans. Animals feel contentment, joy, sadness, excitement, love, anger, jealousy, and more. They express their emotions in the physical world through body language and vocalizations, and telepathically through thoughts and shared feelings. Humans do the same; however, we have developed complex systems of communication that include a variety of spoken languages, the written word, and art.

We can learn about the way animals communicate through careful observation. Numerous studies have been and are being conducted that are discovering insightful details about the animal kingdom. Recently, *National Geographic* published an article about a study that focused on dolphins. It revealed that they use signature whistles, which are similar to names, to call to one another, as well as group vocalizations and unique responses.[4]

---

4   Christine Dell'Amore, "Dolphins Have 'Names,' Respond When Called," *National Geographic,* July 22, 2013, http://news.nationalgeographic.com/news/2013/07/130722-dolphins-whistle-names-identity-animals-science/.

Studies such as this help us to understand the psyches of animals. Attentive observation, scientific studies, research, compassion, patience, and divine love are all ways in which we can delve into the world of animals to discover the rich and plentiful gifts that they bring to our existence on earth.

Communicating with Animals

Each person on this planet was born with the gift of being able to communicate with one another through the spirit. The more in tune you are with your gifts and your love of the animal world, the easier it will be to discern the communications that come from animals. Through patient observation, the use of accurate reference books that provide details about habitats and environments, and knowledgeable resources, including your own intuition and spiritual gifts, you can learn how to read the behaviors of animals, as well as how to communicate with them in an extrasensory manner. People who are gifted with especially strong telepathic communication skills, such as sensitives, empaths, psychics, and mediums, are more apt to pick up on the subtle nuances of animal communication. I will note, though, that it takes an extra dose of compassion, empathy, and patience, as well as a strong desire to learn, in order to truly comprehend what is going on inside the hearts and minds of animals.

Body Language Speaks Volumes

As with people, body language divulges a wealth of information regarding what is going on inside of an animal's mind. Observing the behavior of pets is easiest, because you are around them every day and get to see and experience their actions and reactions to various stimuli. Animals in the wild can also be studied in depth; however, it takes a significant amount of dedication and time to be on location to learn about their behaviors.

With your pets, look at how they walk, how they interact with people and other animals, and the activities that fill their days. Here are a few simple behavioral examples with cats and dogs:

♥ Does your dog lift its head and wag its tail quickly back and forth when a particular neighbor drops by, or does it drop its tail, lower its ears, and growl low in its throat? The wagging of the tail indicates eagerness on the part of your dog to greet your neighbor, while growling is a defensive tactic used to warn the neighbor that their presence is intruding upon the dog's territory.

♥ Does your cat walk around with its tail up in a sort of question mark shape and its head up, or does it drag its tail behind it, so low that the tip almost touches the ground, while furtively looking left and right? When a cat's tail is up and slightly curved at the end, it is an indication of joy and happiness. When a cat is casting darting glances at its surroundings with its tail low to the ground, it could be that it is nervous or anxious about something in its environment, such as another animal that is perceived as a threat. The cat is cautiously scanning the area for the presence of the source of their anxiety.

All animals display physical indicators through their eyes and body language that are specific to the various species. Many of nature's beloved creatures, such as birds, dolphins, cats, dogs, snakes, and frogs, use vocalizations or sounds to further express themselves. By building relationships with the animals within your environment, you can learn about the ways they express themselves, as well as what they are attempting to communicate to you and other animals in their vicinity.

Animals Can Communicate Telepathically

When I communicate telepathically with living animals, it is similar to the manner in which animals communicate with me from heaven. They send me images, thoughts, and feelings. As I mentioned before, the thoughts they send are in a language that I comprehend. It is the language of the spirit that speaks and automatically translates the thoughts into words that are comprehensible to me. The same type of translation occurs when I send my thoughts or speak directly to them. The communication exchange is based upon the connection we have with all spirit. It comes from the heart of our spirits and speaks to the heart of the recipients' spirits. If you have been gifted with strong mediumship skills, diligent practice and confident belief in the talents you possess will increase your natural abilities to communicate with all spirits. In order to transmit and receive messages from living animals, utilize all of your metaphysical senses as you would when communicating with angels or human beings who have crossed over into heaven. Animals will communicate with you when you are tuned in to the heart of their spirits.

♥

Signs Sent by Heaven through the Animal Kingdom

Animals are fantastic creatures. They teach us so much through their behaviors and unconditional love. The American Indians, who have devotedly studied animals for spiritual and sustenance purposes, appreciate the subtle nuances of the behavior of animals. Often, they adopt the spirit of a particular animal as their totem, or guardian. They strongly believe that the spirits of all of the creatures on earth were sent to us as protectors and guides that carry messages of import, which they communicate through behavioral signs and intuitive communication through their spirits.

Spiritually Relevant

In today's world, we no longer have to survive off the land as the American Indians once did centuries ago. Modern inventions and conveniences have moved us away from total immersion in nature; however, that does not mean that the spiritual world of animals is no longer relevant. The animal kingdom is as important today as it was during the time when American Indians roamed the lands unconfined by government-imposed boundaries. Animals continue to provide us with spiritual guidance and information, as well as unconditional love.

Learning about the Animal Kingdom

We can learn about the spiritual signs and messages sent to us by animals through our own telepathic communications and gentle observations, as well as from books that carry the knowledge of those who have studied the animal kingdom in-depth. To start your journey into the world of animals, I recommend the book *Animal Speak* by Ted Andrews. His strong references to the Native American way of life lend credence to his observations about the natural behaviors and spiritual meanings of animals that make their presence known in your life. Guidebooks about the habitats and behaviors of animals will also help you to identify and learn about the characteristics of the different genera and species.

Birds Are Incredible Messengers

All animals have spiritual messages to share with us; however, birds hold a special distinction as incredible messengers of spiritual information for us. The ability of birds to quickly travel by air from one destination to another is symbolic of the swiftness at which spiritual information flows between all spirits. It is interesting to note that the angels, as well as the most well-known messengers in mythology—the Greek god Hermes and the Roman god Mercury—are commonly depicted as having wings. Flight is often associated with the freedom to travel to great heights, which is why birds often carry the messages of greatest import to us.

Each bird has its own symbolic meaning that is based on its habitat and geographical location, its physical characteristics, and its behavior. Birding books and guidebooks hold a treasure trove of information that can help you to identify the various types of birds you encounter around the world. When a particular bird comes into your life, it is sending you a message.

As an example, in the northeastern United States, robins are often seen as a sign of spring. That is because they traditionally appear around that time; however, they may remain year-long residents in certain locales due to environmental conditions that are conducive to their lifestyle. When you see one, and especially if you see many in a short time, it may be a sign of a new beginning or period of growth that is entering your life. The rusty red on its chest may also be symbolic of the sacral chakra, which is associated with the color orange and is located approximately two inches below the belly button. The sacral chakra and the season of spring are often associated with fertility. This may indicate the entrance or renewal of a sexual relationship in your life, or that you will soon be welcoming new additions to your life in the form of children or pets. The symbolism of fertility may also indicate the birth of a new project or the flow of abundance into your life. The abundance may take the form of love, money, time, or opportunities.

Birds, as well as other members of the animal kingdom, may have additional meanings for you that are directly derived from your personal experiences and information that you have learned.

Personal Signs and Messages

In addition to using reference books as a starting point for learning about the animal kingdom, I encourage you to think about what particular animals, birds, reptiles, fish, and insects mean to you. Your heavenly support team frequently uses the natural world to send you important signs and symbols to guide you on your path. Your personal signs and messages will always carry more significance than definitions that come from outside of yourself. For instance, for me, cardinals are always a positive sign about events that are currently unfolding or will occur in the near future. This is because I have historically experienced positive events whenever a cardinal has made an appearance in my life. Blue jays, on the other hand, indicate potential trouble swooping down. Blue jays are very protective and aggressively guard their nests by attacking any perceived threat. They have been known to attack cats, birds, and small predators. They are a sign to me that I should be on guard and remain aware that a negative situation could have an impact on my life. Additionally, their presence is a reminder to pay close attention to my surroundings and the behavior of those around me, as a person or situation may be attempting to upset the balance in my life. I also need to pay attention to what it is that I am doing, as I may be heading in the wrong direction, and the blue jay is giving me a warning to be attentive to the actions I am taking.

Cardinals and blue jays may hold different meanings for you due to your own experiences. If you are unsure of what the presence of a particular bird or other animal means, then that is a good time to pull out your reference books to look up its spiritual meaning. If you cannot find a spiritual meaning for a particular animal, I recommend learning about the natural habitats and behaviors of the animal, for this will give you clues about the message that animal is trying to send you. Use your observation skills and intuition to further define the message that is being sent.

Not Just in Nature

As you become more aware of the presence of nature in your life, as well as the spiritual messages that nature is trying to communicate to you, you may begin to see that the signs of nature can also be found in objects created by humankind. Photographs, drawings, and written words that contain references to nature, such as an image of a fox on the side of a truck or textual references in articles about a particular animal that stand out to you, could be a sign or a message for you. With regard to the fox, it may be that you need to handle a situation with the cleverness of a fox. Pay close attention to what you were thinking about the moment you received the sign, because that is the topic for which you are receiving your answer. If you are repeatedly seeing the same animal over and over again, do your research about the animal in order to figure out the meaning of the message that you are receiving from heaven. Repeated signs and themes mean that spirit is doing its best to get your attention in order to provide answers to questions related to your heart's desires and dreams.

Deep Respect and Gratitude

The deep respect and appreciation that the American Indians have for nature and her creatures demonstrates many lessons for us in this modern world that are still relevant today. All of nature is a gift that we should appreciate and nurture, as its very presence is what sustains our lives. Beyond the most basic factor of ensuring our survival, there is the deep well of knowledge that is passed on to us by nature that feeds our spirits, as well.

I would like to encourage you to enjoy with gratitude, honor, and respect the special blessings that the animal kingdom bestows upon us. As beings created by the loving hand of God, all of us are connected in spirit. As we learn to live in harmony and look beneath the surface of what appears to be, we can recognize and appreciate the assistance we are receiving from heaven through the wonders of the animal kingdom.

♥

Meditating with Nature

Spending time in nature is a wonderful way to rejuvenate and reconnect with your spirit. The fresh air, birds, animals, plants, water, and trees provide you with a panorama of natural beauty that speaks to the heart of your spirit.

Parks and Wildlife Sanctuaries

Parks and wildlife sanctuaries are wonderful places to commune with nature. They have been created and set aside to preserve and protect the natural habitats of the earth. When we visit them, we are there not only to enjoy them, but also to preserve them. It is important to note that the respect that is extended toward nature in the parks and sanctuaries should also be applied toward all flora and fauna of this earth. It is Mother Nature's bounty that provides us with life-giving sustenance, as well as divine guidance, companionship, and natural healing that soothes our souls.

When you go to a park or wildlife sanctuary to commune with nature, take along binoculars to get a good look at the birds, plants, and animals that you discover along your path. Sturdy, but comfortable, footwear and a bottle of water are also recommended. You may also want to bring along a pen and paper to record your thoughts or draw what you see, or bring a camera to visually capture the beauty of what you are experiencing.

Observe the Beauty

When you are exploring the world of nature as a method of meditating, have no expectations other than to breathe in the fresh air and to take delight in the sights and sounds that nature offers. Take note of the way the sun filters through the trees or sparkles as it reflects off of the water of a stream or lake. Listen to the music of the birds as they sing to one another in the trees. To see the animals, such as deer and foxes, the best time to visit is near dawn or dusk, as this is when they venture out to forage for food. Most of all, respect the homes and habitats of the animals by simply being an observer. Do not destroy or disturb their environment or leave litter behind. We can all be good citizens of this earth by respecting nature and our environment. Be there to enjoy the splendor of the earth and to breathe in the peace that comes from observing nature's simplicity, beauty, and innocence. It is a gift worth preserving. For those of you who are already actively respecting and maintaining the environment in both large and small ways, know that Mother Nature sends you her gratitude.

Step Outside

Nature can be enjoyed at any time. You do not need to be at a park to hear the birds or to walk barefoot in the grass. Nature is all around us every day. It is in the air we breathe, the water we drink, the vegetables and plants we eat, and the flowers we grow, as well as in the pets we graciously open our homes and hearts to, the rabbits that hop in our yards, the bees that propagate the pollen for the plants, and the sun that brings warmth and light to our world.

Whenever you need to feel refreshed and rejuvenated, go outside and take a deep breath. Thank Mother Nature for the gifts she grants you and reconnect with the spirit that is within the heart of your soul.

♥

The Power of the Ocean

Every aspect of the ocean not only offers a delight for the senses, but also teaches us valuable lessons for the growth of our spirits. There is a special kind of magic that comes from the ocean. Its powerful currents, magnificent creatures, and wondrous waters provide the rhythmic heartbeat of the earth, insight with respect to the fluidity of life, and a cleansing energy that refreshes our spirits.

The Calming Pulse of the Ocean

The sound of the ocean waves continuously rolling in and pulling back from the shore is soothing in its rhythm, like a mother's heartbeat is to her children. It is a comforting and peaceful sound that can be mimicked within our own bodies when we breathe deeply in meditation. While breathing in deeply through your nose and slowly releasing your breath through your nose or your mouth, listen to the sound of your breath. Physically feel the calming pulse of the ocean as it washes through your body in the form of your breath and envision the waves that match the cadence of your breathing. Becoming aware of the breath of life that flows through you synchronizes you with the positive, life-giving energies of the earth and centers you in the moment. By giving yourself the gift of this meditation, you are allowing your spirit to cleanse itself of negative or unwanted energies. Worries and concerns dissipate, opening your heart and mind to the welcoming and positive energies that provide your spirit the freedom to follow its path to its true heart's desires.

Perform this breathing meditation with no expectation other than to find your center and to feel the peace and calm that rests within your soul. Acknowledge any thoughts that crop up in your mind, thank them for their presence, and allow them to drift away as you refocus on your breath and the power of the ocean that flows through you.

You can utilize this method of meditation for both short sessions of a minute or two and long sessions of up to thirty minutes or more. The choice is yours. Be sure to have a quiet space in which to practice your meditations by turning off all electronic devices and eliminating any distractions that could come from pets, children, friends, roommates, colleagues, or other sources. A quiet environment will allow you to truly step into your own meditation space and connect with the spirit that is within you.

What the Creatures of the Ocean Teach Us

The creatures of the ocean teach us spiritual lessons about the application of adaptability and fluidity in response to the circumstances that we encounter. Oceanic creatures glide through water, a much heavier substance than air, with grace and ease. As humans on a spiritual journey, our lives on earth are much like time spent in dense water compared to the lighter air we experience in heaven. While here, we can adapt to the heavier atmosphere of earth by learning to move with the currents of life, rather than resisting the experiences that assist us with the lessons we have chosen for this lifetime. By doing so, we are giving our higher selves permission to accept that all circumstances, whether negative or positive, are important to the development of our souls.

Remember to Play

The dolphins of the seas take the lesson of adaptability and fluidity one step further by teaching us the importance of working and playing together. Establishing a balance within your own life, as well as within the relationships you have with others, directly addresses your own feelings of worthiness to receive, as well as to give. Our lives are not meant to be a long road of unhappiness or unpleasant circumstances. The choices and decisions that you make determine your destiny. External circumstances do affect you; however, it is entirely up to you to decide how you are going to react and what actions you will take.

Carving out time to play is as important to your soul as scheduling time to work on important projects. It is a form of meditation that allows us to see with the eyes of a child again. It helps us to release our cares and worries, and opens up the world of our imaginations. The joy and happiness that you invite into your life will also free up your mind to discover solutions and ideas. People who work in creative careers know that ideas need positive stimulation and an open mind in order to come forth and develop into something meaningful. Taking the time to play may be just what is needed to free your mind of a problem or obstacle you are facing at work or home. Hand your worries and concerns over to the angels while you play. They will work on providing solutions during this time. Answers may be presented to you in the form of an epiphany or idea that seems to come to you out of the blue.

Spiritually Cleansing Waters

The wondrous waters of the ocean contain an element that truly cleanses our spirits of any unwanted or negative energies. As we go throughout our days, we knowingly and unknowingly pick up energies from the people, objects, and environment around us. The unpalatable waters of the ocean do not slake our thirst or cleanse our physical bodies without special treatment, but they do provide a beautiful cleansing of spirit. In a way, it is as if the ocean collects all of the salty tears that we have cried and removes the sadness that pervades our souls from time to time.

By immersing ourselves in the ocean, we can utilize its energies to wash away the disappointments of the past and bring forth new experiences. As the ocean draws the water back into itself, a new wave is there, ready to take its place. Each wave is different, too. Some are large and powerful, while others are gentle swells that roll in to the shore. It is the same with our life experiences. Some changes can alter the landscapes of our lives, while other transitions are smooth and gliding. We can learn to love and appreciate all of the waves in our lives through meaningful observation, which helps us to gauge the strength of the situations we encounter, as well as through the open acceptance of the inevitability of change that leads to growth.

Imagine Yourself There

Even if you do not have the opportunity to be near the ocean, you can always use your imagination to hear the sounds and feel the cleansing power of its waters. Seashells, saltwater fish, and images of the creatures of the sea are all wonderful representations of the ocean that you can place in your environment as a reminder of the lessons that Mother Nature teaches you through her seas. Relax and enjoy her gifts to you with gratitude, appreciation, and love.

♥

Crystals:
Treasures of the Earth

Crystals are more than just pretty rocks that are cut into shapes for jewelry or placed on bookshelves to bring color to a room. Each crystal holds unique energies that can be utilized for healing, for gridding a sacred space, to provide protective or strengthening energies, to enhance your own energies, and to cleanse energies.

Eager to Learn

As a child, I had always been drawn to crystals and stones, and frequently asked my father to help me identify the ones I found in our yard and in nature. By the time I reached my teenage years, I had discovered from books that crystals have special properties. At the time, I did not know what those spiritual properties were; however, I knew I wanted to learn more.

The very first crystal that I was immediately drawn to, and ended up purchasing, was a clear quartz crystal that hung around my neck and over my heart chakra. Soon after purchasing it, I picked up a copy of

Love Is in the Earth by Melody, which is a great reference book for looking up the spiritual meanings of crystals. From the book, I learned that clear quartz is one of the most versatile crystals with regard to its properties and strengths. My crystal collection has grown considerably since that time, and to this day, *Love Is in the Earth* is one of the many books I use to look up the properties of the various crystals I collect and love.

How to Select the Best Crystal for You

When collecting crystals, whether you find them in nature or purchase them in stores, I recommend selecting the stones toward which you are drawn. It is always a wonderful delight to go home and look up the spiritual properties of the crystals I have found. Most of the time, the meaning of the crystal or the energies that it emits are exactly what I can benefit from in my life. As a note, the value of purchasing rather than finding crystals is that they are already clearly marked and identified for you. When you locate a crystal in nature, it can sometimes be difficult to ascertain what you have found. Unless it is an easily identifiable or common stone, you may have to consult with a geologist because several crystals look alike but are structurally unique and contain very different energetic properties. Special tests can be performed by professionals to identify the type of crystal you have found.

As you page through your reference books, you may come across a crystal that you would love to add to your collection because it has energies that would assist you or someone else with a particular life situation. This is another way to find crystals; however, it may lead you on a very interesting and adventurous hunt if the crystal is hard to find or obtain. There are times when it has taken me a few years to find a specific crystal that I had been looking for—it may have been due to its rarity, or because the timing was not right for me to find it. I do believe that crystals come into our lives for a reason. That is why I recommend letting them find you by using the methodology of picking up or purchasing the ones you are drawn toward instead of searching them out. If specific energy provided by a crystal is needed or strongly desired, it will make an appearance in your life when the timing is right.

Different Crystals Require Different Care

Crystals can be porous or solid, as well as fragile or strong. It is important to know the various properties of your crystal before you attempt to cleanse it, because you may end up ruining or damaging it if you use the wrong substance to rid it of dust, dirt, or accumulated energies that need to be removed.

Crystals both emit and collect energy. As a crystal works to bring you healing or lend you its energies, it may be collecting and accumulating energies from its surroundings. In light of that, it is a good idea to regularly cleanse your crystals of any unwanted or negative energies they have picked up from their environment. While looking up the spiritual properties of your crystal, pay close attention to its physical properties. Reference books often provide excellent advice for the care and maintenance of each crystal in your collection. For instance, some crystals can be cleansed or recharged with salt water or sunlight, while others would disintegrate or fade under such treatments. One of my favorite methods for cleansing crystals of negative or unwanted energies is to smudge them with dried white sage.

Smudging Crystals, Your Home, and You

Smudging is the act of using the smoke of a dried plant to capture and dissipate any unwanted or negative energies that have accumulated on or within objects, environments, and people. For centuries, the element of air in the form of smoke has been used in rituals for purifying. I have always used dried white sage that is bundled with string, also referred to as a smudging stick, to perform my own cleansing practices. Dried white sage is well known for its cleansing properties and can be purchased at many New Age stores, as well as on the Internet.

A Method for Smudging

1. Open a door or window to allow an avenue for the smoke and negative or unwanted energies to leave the environment.

2. Choose a special bowl, container, or large bowl-like seashell to use as an ash catcher, as well as to extinguish the sage when you have completed your smudging.

3. Carefully ignite the sage with a lighter or matches. As you would with incense, gently blow out the flame and allow the sage to smolder and release its smoke. Keep your ash-catching container with you as you smudge to capture any errant ashes that may fall from the dried white sage or smudging stick.

4. Call upon your heavenly support team to assist you with the cleansing of your crystals, house, or person. Thank them for assisting you with your task.

5. State your intention to cleanse the specific object, environment, or person of any negative or unwanted energies, as well as to infuse the object, space, or person with positive energies and love. This can be said silently in your mind or spoken out loud.

6. For your home or other structures, go through each room, repeating your intentions while gently waving the smoke throughout the entire room, including the corners. It is a good practice to cleanse your entire house, including the attic and basement (if you have them), at least once a month. In between the whole-house smudging, I recommend cleansing the main rooms at least once a week. Once you have completed the ritual, wave the smoke out of the open door or window to sweep the negative or unwanted energies out of your environment.

7. For crystals, cleanse all sides of the crystal, if possible, while stating your intentions. When you purchase or obtain new crystals, it is a good idea to cleanse them before using them or carrying them on your person. Periodically cleanse your crystals, especially if you frequently use them, wear them, or carry them. In addition, if you use them for healing or crystal layouts, cleanse them immediately afterward to remove any energies they may have picked up in the healing process.

8. For yourself or another person, sweep the smoke around the body as you state your intentions. This can be done in a standing position with arms extended to the sides of the body at shoulder height. If this is not possible, as in the case of someone who is bedridden, the smoke can be carefully drifted over the body. Move your bowl with the sage so as not to drop any ash on the person or any flammable objects.

9. If the sage stops smoldering and releasing smoke while you are smudging, re-light it and continue on with the process from where you left off.

10. When you have completed your cleansing, carefully snuff out the smoldering sage in your bowl, container, or shell.

11. Thank your heavenly support team for their assistance and their blessings.

Usually, after I have cleansed a space or myself, I experience a feeling of lightness and peace. Routine smudging is a good practice to establish to prevent the building up of negative or unwanted energies. As it becomes more routine, you will feel a noticeable difference when you forget to cleanse, as your environment will feel heavier or you will experience an increase in negative feelings.

Enjoy the Energy

The energy of the earth that pulses within crystals is here for us to utilize in a responsible manner and with enjoyment. Crystals are one of the treasures of the earth that are available to us for the purposes of healing and soul evolvement. Enjoy the beauty, the unique properties, and the positive energies that they can lend to your daily existence and life purpose.

Reiki Energy Healing

Reiki energy healing is a natural restorative that attunes us to the great love within our spirits that comes from our Creator. Reiki was rediscovered by Dr. Mikao Usui in Japan and brought to the United States by Hawayo Takada, one of his students. It is a form of energy healing that works through the light of God's love that is within each of us. Its purpose is to realign our minds, bodies, and spirits to a perfect state of being.

A Brief Explanation of Reiki Application

Reiki is administered by a practitioner who has been trained in the art of drawing the healing energy of God through his or her spirit and into yours. For a recipient of Reiki, it is as relaxing as a massage, even though the light touch involved in the administering of Reiki does not compare to the level of touch involved in the application of a massage. In a standard session, the practitioner gently places cupped hands upon the head, neck, shoulders, arms, stomach, outer hips, legs, and feet. For the energy centers of the heart, as well as the sacral and root chakras, which are in the areas of the abdomen and the tail bone, Reiki energy can be transferred with the hands held several inches away from the body or through another area in order to maintain the dignity and respect of the recipient and the practitioner. Unlike a massage, Reiki energy can also be sent over distances, which requires no touch. In my experience, the most effective session is when the energy is transferred in person by the practitioner to the recipient.

Receiving Reiki Energy

As the recipient of a Reiki treatment, you do not have to believe in its power in order for it to work. The positive energy will flow through you and provide healing, regardless of your thought processes. However, you will certainly get much more out of your session if you keep an open mind and graciously accept the healing light and energy of God.

As a note, you may have a specific intention for your healing session, such as relieving the pain of a headache or clearing your energy centers of negativity. You can tell your practitioner of your intention, and you can hold it in your mind as the practitioner provides you with energy healing. The energy itself will flow wherever it is needed, though, whether you have stated an intention or not.

As a practitioner, it is not a usual practice for me to hold a specific intention for healing in my mind, because the energy will flow where it is needed. I will say, though, that I have performed sessions in which

I have targeted specific ailments for recipients or for myself. In these cases, it was not practical to perform a full Reiki session. Instead of waiting for the perfect time and place, I directly apply Reiki to a specific area to assist with the removal of pain from a headache or other minor affliction.

Many applications of Reiki for minor ailments of the body, mind, or spirit usually require one session on an occasional basis, while other, more complicated conditions may require multiple Reiki sessions. These conditions include the treatments for arthritis, tumors, chronic back pain, or deep emotional or spiritual pain.

Natural Reactions

As you let the Reiki energy flow through you, you may drift off to sleep or enter into a meditative or dream-like state in which you experience visions. These are natural reactions to the relaxing and positive energy that is flowing throughout your spirit. Additionally, you may feel the energy as it streams from the practitioner and into you. The way it feels may differ for each person and practitioner, as well as per session, due to the way the energy is being applied to the mind, body, and spirit. As an example of what it may feel like, one of the recipients of a Reiki healing session I provided mentioned to me that my energy felt like a soft, falling rain that soothed the body and the soul.

Not a Replacement for Traditional Medical Treatments

As wonderful as Reiki is, I recommend that you use it as an accompaniment to traditional medical treatments, and not as a replacement. There have been many wonderful advancements in the field of medicine for many serious diseases. As with musicians, angels work as invisible muses for scientists and doctors as they devise new treatments and cures for the human body. By combining Reiki with traditional medicine, you are treating not only the physical body, but also the mind and the spirit.

How to Become a Reiki Practitioner

In order to become a Reiki practitioner, you need to learn firsthand from a Reiki master. It is a tradition that is passed on from person to person, and cannot be learned from books. There are books out there that contain a lot of information about Reiki; however, there are omissions to the content, as this practice was once held as a closely guarded secret that was only passed down to a select few. Today, the practice has become more widespread; therefore, it is easier to find a master who is willing to teach you the precepts of Reiki. A person who has achieved the level of Reiki master is one who has completed all three levels of Reiki training, which enables them to pass on their skills to others. As with any topic that you decide to study, Reiki should be approached with respect and honor for your teachers, or sensei, as well as for the topic itself.

Types of Healing

There are many forms of Reiki, as well as other methods of energy healing. One is not better than the other, as they all have the same goal and intention—to realign your spirit to the light that is within all of us. Whichever methodology you choose for your healing will be the right one for you.

We Are One

Connected by Love

We are the garden of God's soul. When he created each of our spirits out of the energy of his love, he planted a seed within our souls with the hope and expectation that we would grow and evolve into the beautiful creations he meant us to be. God is non-denominational and non-gender specific, as are the angels. It does not matter what name you call him or her, whether it is God, the Creator, Allah, or Yahweh, because the Creator is the embodiment of all of creation and names are only labels that we use as a convenient means of identifying and communicating our thoughts about the beings, objects, and energies of the world. Ultimately, God is love. Every aspect of the universe is born out of the energy of God's love. It is what binds us together in spirit and unites us as one with each other and him.

His greatest aspiration for us is to be as love—to live it, to share it, to receive it, to recognize it, to appreciate it, and to exult within its glorious energy and power. In doing so, we are living extensions of the love that is him.

Our Incredible Connection

We are incredibly interconnected with one another through the light of our souls, which has been given to us by God. That light connects us to all animals, all plants, every element on earth, and every being in the universe, including spirit in heaven and beyond. We all originated from the same source, with the same energy. Due to the connection we have with one another, when we bring pain to another soul, we are hurting ourselves and we are hurting God. When we love ourselves, one another, and God, we are the living embodiment of our life purposes. That is why, when we cross over into heaven and review our lives, the most important question that we will answer is: How have you loved? It is the reason we were created and what we are meant to rediscover on our journey as human beings on earth, as well as in spirit in heaven.

Each day, more and more souls are reawakening to the light within them. They are realizing that there is more to life than what can be seen, felt, heard, tasted, and smelled with the ordinary senses that we use each day on the surface of our human existence. The light of God's love that energizes our spirits allows us to see beyond the ordinary to experience the extraordinary and to truly know what it means to love.

Cosmic Shift

We are currently living in a time in which we have the potential to experience a cosmic shift in consciousness across the world. With each soul that reawakens to the light of his or her spirit, the light and love in the world grows exponentially stronger and the illusion of darkness and negativity recedes as the veil is lifted from our souls. Our strength is in our love, and it has the potential to reclaim the world with its peace. It starts with one soul at a time ... and today, that beautiful soul could be you.

My Prayer for You

It is my hope and prayer that the words I have lovingly shared with you have helped you to wake up to the light that is within you. You are the perfect creation and child of God. You have been forged in love, guided by love, and are love. May your life be a shining example of the love that exists within all of our spirits, and may you experience the divine joy of heaven on earth.

Afterword

Thank you for reading *How Have You Loved?*

It was my intention in writing it to share with you the knowledge I have gained and the experiences I have lived through, in order to shed light on the reason we are here and what we can do to experience the brilliance of our souls while we are living our lives on earth.

You, as well as all spirits, are my inspiration. Thank you for the light and love that we share, as well as for the beautiful spirit that is you.

With light and love from my spirit to yours,
Karen T. Hluchan
Spirit Medium & Reiki Master

www.HealingSpiritWithLove.com

Acknowledgments

I am eternally grateful for the role that spirits in heaven have played in the writing of *How Have You Loved?* I admire and wonder at the fantastic way that you orchestrate the events of my life, as well as the lives of every being on earth. It is your divine beauty and light that shines through the words and the pages. Thank you for your love, support, inspiration, and guidance.

My mother, Janice Hluchan, has been a tremendous help through her belief in me and my abilities, as well as through her diligent dedication to the proofreading of my writing. Her honest feedback and sharp eye for detail were an invaluable asset to the development of the content of *How Have You Loved?* Thank you, Mom, for being a wonderful example of the living, shining proof of all that is good in this world. The light of your soul will always be remembered in the hearts of all who have met you and have yet to meet you.

To my sister, Robyn Hluchan; my brother, Geoff Friel; and my best friend, Elizabeth Price, thank you for your love and support, as well as for all of the lessons we have learned together. Through the challenges we all have faced, we have maintained our friendship and respect for one another. I am glad that we are making the journey through this lifetime together.

To my most intimate of soul groups, which includes my closest friends and family both here and in heaven, your encouragement, interest, and support mean the world to me. It is an honor to know you, and I thank you for all of the love you share with me each and every day.

To Joshua Barber, thank you for the part you played in my reawakening. Spirit orchestrated our meeting in a way that I will never forget. Thank you for your loving support, as well as for our long chats in person and on the phone. You are a fabulous friend and a beautiful spirit. Thank you for being you!

To Emmanuel and Elia, meeting you meant more to me than you know. The gift you gave me was sent directly from God through you. Your love is an inspiration, as is your presence here on earth. You may not know this, Emmanuel, but it was your first book, *Bring Forth the Light*, that introduced me to the existence of Balboa Press and provided encouragement for my dreams of being a published author. Thank you so much for sharing your gifts and love with me and the world.

To James Van Praagh, John Holland, José Gosschalk, Tony Stockwell, and Marilyn Whall, thank you for providing the last piece of the puzzle that I needed to recognize how I see as a medium. I am honored to have met you and to have learned more about my gifts through workshops with you. International Mediumship Week at the Omega Institute was one of the best experiences of my life. Thank you for the love and light that you shine in this world!

To the Omega Institute, thank you for providing a beautiful and spiritually enriching environment for the growth of all of our souls. I am grateful for the time I spent on your campus expanding my skills and meeting wonderful people who walk within the light.

To Dwight O'Neal at Balboa Press, the first day you called me regarding my inquiry about publishing a book was magical. It was as though there was an angel on the other end of the line. Your encouragement and belief that I would complete my book sooner than I thought gave me the spark I needed to do just that. Thank you for your inspiration and belief in me!

To Louise L. Hay, Hay House Publishing, and Balboa Press, thank you for providing a means for me, and other authors like me, to share our love with the world by publishing the words written by the heart of our spirits. Namaste!

To all of the people that I have met and known in my life, thank you for your presence, the lessons learned, the experiences we shared, and the love. Every experience in my life has contributed to the contents of *How Have You Loved?*, which makes you an integral part of its contents. Thank you for the roles you have played in my life, whether they were positive or seemingly negative experiences, because every circumstance has enabled me to be who I am today. I share with you the love of my heart. Let your light shine!

To all spirit on earth, in heaven, and beyond, thank you for your love. I acknowledge your spirit with the light of my own, and I thank you for the opportunity to give and receive the greatest gift we have ever been given—love.

Bibliography

Andrews, Ted. *Animal Speak.* Woodbury, Minnesota: Llewellyn Publications, 1993.

Bryan, Charles W. "What are Dreams." *How Stuff Works, a Discovery Company.* Retrieved June, 27, 2013. http://science.howstuffworks.com/life/what-are-dreams.htm.

Day, Laura. *Practical Intuition: How to Harness the Power of Your Instinct and Make It Work for You.* New York: Broadway Books, 1996.

Dell'Amore, Christine. "Dolphins Have 'Names,' Respond When Called." *National Geographic,* July 22, 2013. http://news.nationalgeographic.com/news/2013/07/130722-dolphins-whistle-names-identity-animals-science/.

Holland, John. *101 Ways to Jump-Start Your Intuition.* Carlsbad, California: Hay House, Inc., 2005.

Melody. *Love Is in the Earth: A Kaleidoscope of Crystals.* Wheat Ridge, Colorado: Earth-Love Publishing House, 1995.

Rand, William Lee. "What Is the History of Reiki?" *The International Center for Reiki Training.* Retrieved July 29, 2013. http://www.reiki.org/faq/historyofreiki.html.

Van Biema, David. "Mother Theresa's Crisis of Faith." *Time Magazine*, August 23, 2007. http://www.time.com/time/magazine/article/0,9171,1655720,00.html.

Virtue, Doreen. *Archangels 101: How to Connect Closely with Archangels Michael, Raphael, Gabriel, Uriel, and Others for Healing, Protection, and Guidance.* Carlsbad, California: Hay House, Inc., 2001.

Zerner, Amy and Monty Farber. *The Enchanted Tarot.* New York: St. Martin's Press, 1990.

Index

A

abilities 9, 117, 121, 125, 137, 138, 174, 180, 182, 192, 227

ability 77, 93, 102, 126, 137, 166, 194

absolute faith 75, 76, 77, 78, 79

absolute trust 67, 75, 79

abstract 114, 119, 120, 158

abstract puzzle 114

abundance 17, 31, 45, 51, 52, 53, 63, 69, 75, 101, 195

acceptance 75, 76, 78, 92, 154, 205

accident 62, 84, 109, 180

accomplishment 34, 40, 41, 42, 171

acknowledgement 113

action iv, xiii, 4, 9, 10, 11, 12, 16, 17, 21, 25, 27, 32, 33, 35, 40, 43, 47, 49, 56, 65, 73, 89, 105, 123, 151, 152, 163, 167, 173, 177, 178, 191, 196, 204

addiction 173

advice iv, 47, 70, 94, 103, 104, 123, 134, 209

Akashic Record 60, 65

AI 54, 55, 56, 57, 58

Allah 221

all-knowing 120, 121

All You Need is Love 159

Alzheimer's 87

angelic assistance 86

Angels xii, 5, 6, 7, 10, 15, 16, 17, 19, 21, 22, 25, 29, 31, 33, 35, 41, 47, 48, 59, 60, 61, 62, 63, 65, 67, 68, 69, 72, 73, 74, 75, 76, 83, 85, 87, 89, 95, 96, 109, 110, 119, 122, 124, 127, 138, 139, 140, 142, 145, 148, 149, 168, 172, 173, 174, 177, 179, 181, 182, 185, 186, 192, 194, 205, 217, 221

Angels on Earth 177, 179

animal communication 190

animal kingdom 189, 193, 194, 196, 198

animals 34, 35, 96, 99, 100, 137, 180, 189, 190, 191, 192, 193, 194, 196, 199, 200, 222, 231

Animal Speak 194, 231

answer xiii, 10, 17, 21, 26, 29, 31, 48, 49, 63, 64, 75, 96, 106, 107, 127, 129, 136, 139, 145, 146, 147, 151, 157, 158, 165, 167, 179, 184, 185, 197, 205, 222

anxiety 13, 32, 94, 191

appreciate 10, 15, 30, 35, 40, 42, 53, 58, 65, 88, 123, 124, 130, 147, 171, 181, 193, 198, 205, 221

appreciation 18, 29, 34, 35, 41, 124, 181, 198, 206

Archangels 60, 62, 232

architect 95

aroma 118, 134, 135

artist 95, 157

ask 5, 6, 7, 10, 15, 25, 39, 41, 43, 47, 48, 51, 52, 53, 61, 63, 64, 66, 68, 69, 73,

74, 75, 78, 103, 106, 107, 108, 122, 123, 131, 138, 142, 146, 149, 168, 174, 184, 185, 186

asking 39, 48, 52, 54, 63, 64, 65, 69, 107, 123, 131, 146, 147

assessment 9

assistance 41, 47, 60, 63, 64, 65, 69, 75, 76, 78, 85, 86, 87, 89, 95, 113, 115, 119, 137, 140, 142, 146, 155, 180, 181, 198, 212

attributes 40, 42, 118, 189

aura 106, 115, 131

awareness 20, 32, 109, 123, 124, 140, 172

B

bad habit 5

balance 17, 50, 51, 52, 53, 54, 58, 196, 204

Beatles 159

behavior xiv, 8, 9, 10, 12, 15, 23, 27, 28, 51, 53, 70, 121, 168, 174, 190, 191, 193, 194, 195, 196, 197

be here now 21

beings v, xiii, xiv, 19, 21, 61, 101, 104, 106, 107, 109, 113, 115, 120, 121, 126, 140, 156, 163, 169, 179, 192, 198, 221, 222

believe 6, 17, 55, 76, 77, 78, 79, 84, 88, 105, 106, 111, 124, 181, 193, 209, 215

best friend 4, 42, 43, 47, 54, 57, 85, 118, 119, 159, 183, 227

birds 99, 144, 156, 191, 194, 195, 196, 199, 200

blame xi, 27, 28

blessing xi, 11, 22, 26, 42, 52, 73, 113, 115, 124, 171, 198, 212

blessing in disguise 11, 73

block 10, 21, 57, 63, 71, 103, 105, 140, 141, 166

body 15, 41, 48, 84, 87, 89, 93, 109, 115, 116, 131, 132, 133, 134, 144, 149, 189, 190, 191, 202, 212, 215, 216, 217

body language 131, 189, 190, 191

breath 40, 116, 143, 201, 202, 203

breathe 41, 48, 200, 202

Buddha 61

butterflies 112, 127

C

celebration 13, 85, 179

Chakra 132, 195, 207, 214

channel 115, 116

characteristic 106, 131, 194, 195

charity 180, 181

child xi, 35, 95, 103, 204, 207, 223

children 20, 21, 34, 61, 76, 95, 100, 180, 195, 202, 203

choice 8, 9, 26, 29, 33, 46, 49, 77, 83, 85, 86, 97, 146, 163, 164, 165, 167, 170, 171, 173, 174, 175, 180, 203, 204

choose 7, 10, 12, 22, 26, 27, 28, 29, 40, 52, 63, 73, 75, 84, 88, 96, 97, 104, 126, 139, 140, 164, 165, 167, 168, 171, 173, 180, 210, 218

choosing 26, 28, 29, 128

chose 18, 166, 171, 184

clairalience 134

clairalient 134

clairambience 135

clairambient 135, 136, 137

clairaudience 127, 130, 133

clairaudient 127

claircognizance 133

claircognizant 134

clairsentience 117, 130, 132

clairsentient 132

clairvoyance 126

clairvoyant 126

clarify 107

cleansing 202, 205, 206, 210, 211, 212

coincidence 139

Collective or Universal Mind 95, 139

coma 88

comatose 87

comfort xii, 15, 30, 39, 59, 67, 69, 71, 89, 96, 97, 99, 101, 102, 109, 113, 177

communicates 101, 114, 180

communication xii, xiv, 10, 11, 62, 63, 70, 83, 85, 94, 95, 101, 102, 105, 106, 108, 113, 114, 115, 116, 119, 121, 122, 123, 124, 127, 134, 136, 137, 145, 182, 183, 185, 186, 189, 190, 192, 193, 194

companionship 199

complex 114, 124, 137, 156, 172, 186, 189

concentrate 33, 48, 103, 115, 116, 152

confidence 7, 73, 79, 171

confident xii, 44, 184, 192

connect 60, 63, 137, 143, 144, 172, 186, 203, 222, 232

connection xiv, 32, 77, 93, 96, 99, 115, 135, 136, 137, 139, 141, 143, 145, 152, 178, 192, 222

consciousness 30, 40, 95, 104, 150, 222

consume 13, 15, 97

contentment 45, 181, 189

control 3, 12, 15, 17, 25, 26, 31, 73, 78, 105, 174

conversation 32, 55, 114, 119, 173, 183, 184, 185

coping 91

cosmic shift 222

counseling 87, 97, 169

co-worker 47, 70

creative 96, 119, 204

Creator xiv, 45, 59, 60, 74, 76, 214, 221

crossed over 85, 87, 94, 95, 100, 112, 192

cross over xii, 58, 83, 84, 85, 86, 88, 89, 91, 99, 100, 113, 222

Crown Chakra 132

crystals 146, 207, 208, 209, 210, 211, 213, 231

D

databank 107, 118, 120, 125, 148, 149

daydreams 31, 63, 95

death 15, 84, 85, 88, 91, 92, 96, 106, 109, 119, 153, 172

Deceased Loved Ones 7, 59, 62, 63, 83, 95, 96, 100, 104, 111, 119, 121, 123, 127, 140, 148, 153, 154, 158

decipher 111, 139, 151, 152

decision xiii, 5, 22, 46, 49, 68, 88, 167, 172, 174, 175, 177, 180, 204

dedication 138, 191, 227

denial 55, 92

depression 50, 53, 93, 100

deserve 4, 6, 17, 44, 89, 123

desire 5, 6, 15, 31, 33, 46, 47, 64, 66, 69, 70, 79, 132, 142, 146, 152, 166, 168, 190, 197, 203

destiny xiv, 21, 204

dimension 87, 113

discipline 138

disease 84, 93, 99, 107, 170, 217

Divine xiv, 46, 63, 76, 77, 115, 120, 122, 123, 190, 199, 223, 227

divine communication 115, 122, 123

divine guidance 46, 199

divine intervention 63

divorce 15

doctor 70, 78, 95, 123, 132, 217

dolphin 189, 191, 204, 231

Don't Stop Believing 128

Doreen Virtue 60

doubt 72, 75, 76, 88, 128, 133

dragonflies 112, 127

dream 3, 5, 6, 7, 16, 17, 21, 24, 26, 29, 32, 33, 42, 44, 46, 48, 49, 62, 66, 67, 69, 70, 71, 72, 73, 74, 75, 79, 87, 88, 95, 96, 139, 148, 149, 150, 151, 152, 153, 154, 155, 164, 166, 169, 172, 173, 179, 181, 197, 216, 228, 231

dream dictionaries 149, 150

dreams 3, 5, 6, 7, 16, 17, 21, 24, 26, 29, 33, 42, 44, 46, 48, 49, 62, 66, 67, 69, 70, 72, 73, 74, 75, 79, 95, 96, 139, 148, 149, 150, 152, 153, 154, 155, 164, 166, 169, 172, 173, 179, 181, 197, 228, 231

Dr. Hluchan 70, 225, 227

E

Earth 4, 5, 6, 8, 12, 35, 40, 49, 50, 61, 62, 66, 77, 78, 83, 84, 85, 86, 87, 88, 89, 90, 91, 93, 94, 95, 96, 97, 98, 99, 100, 101, 103, 104, 105, 106, 109, 113, 116, 117, 124, 125, 126, 132, 135, 136, 137, 141, 154, 156, 163, 165, 169, 170, 171, 172, 173, 176, 177, 179, 180, 181, 190, 193, 199, 200, 202, 203, 204, 207, 208, 213, 222, 223, 225, 227, 228, 229, 231

eating 13, 14, 15, 16, 18, 19, 117

education 61, 71, 123

ego 4, 32, 39, 40, 41, 48, 49, 63, 68, 77, 140, 143, 159, 163, 169, 177

electricity 108

elevate 7, 73, 76, 78, 144, 185

emotion 9, 10, 13, 100, 101, 106, 117, 130, 131, 132, 156, 167, 168, 185, 189

emotional baggage 23

empathy 12, 183, 190

energy 1, 3, 8, 9, 23, 24, 28, 33, 41, 50, 51, 73, 74, 89, 94, 95, 105, 106, 108, 115, 116, 122, 124, 126, 131, 132, 137, 165, 170, 180, 202, 209, 213, 214, 215, 216, 218, 221, 222

energy healing 95, 214, 215, 218

engineer 95

environment 17, 73, 78, 94, 112, 133, 190, 191, 192, 200, 203, 205, 206, 209, 210, 211, 212, 228

epiphanies 63, 95, 154

epiphany 20, 48, 205

error 11, 25

everyday concerns 41, 183

evolution 46, 60, 61, 65, 66, 74, 85, 90, 139, 140, 174

evolve 9, 12, 84, 94, 171, 186, 221

evolvement 8, 12, 23, 24, 49, 60, 77, 85, 96, 97, 163, 170, 172, 173, 213

exercise 5, 15, 18, 33, 35, 41, 47, 63, 76, 79, 117, 126, 132, 133, 141, 151, 152

external signs 10, 31, 32, 48, 62, 63, 112, 115, 127, 141

extrasensory 125, 126, 127, 130, 133, 134, 135, 190

F

faith 16, 17, 19, 46, 49, 65, 67, 68, 72, 73, 75, 76, 77, 78, 79, 182, 232

falling in love 39, 43

family 34, 51, 95, 123, 186, 227

fate 62, 68, 168

father 47, 118, 128, 153, 207

fear 7, 8, 9, 12, 20, 21, 32, 44, 45, 49, 68, 71, 88, 102, 103, 120, 124, 150, 153, 159, 163, 164, 165, 166, 167, 168, 169, 170, 172, 173, 177, 178

feedback 11, 40, 168, 227

feeling 10, 13, 15, 17, 18, 25, 32, 39, 41, 47, 48, 50, 52, 67, 68, 84, 88, 89, 91, 92, 94, 96, 97, 101, 102, 106, 109, 112, 114, 118, 119, 125, 130, 131, 132, 133, 134, 139, 146, 148, 152, 167, 168, 171, 189, 192, 204, 212

finding your center 47, 48, 63, 76, 79

find your center 40, 41, 42, 66, 78, 144, 185, 203

forgive 12, 25, 39, 97

forgiving 23, 24, 25, 44

free will 26, 63, 68, 88, 104, 105, 123, 165, 173

friend 4, 10, 17, 22, 34, 39, 40, 42, 43, 47, 51, 54, 55, 56, 57, 58, 61, 70, 84, 85, 100, 110, 118, 119, 121, 131, 136, 139, 159, 165, 166, 171, 176, 180, 183, 185, 186, 189, 203, 227, 228

G

Gabriel 60, 232

gateway 35, 84, 88, 89, 145

generosity 51

genuine 133, 183, 184, 186

gift xiv, 17, 22, 29, 30, 34, 35, 40, 41, 42, 44, 45, 52, 63, 70, 72, 75, 76, 77, 81, 85, 93, 103, 105, 109, 113, 117, 120, 121, 122, 123, 124, 125, 126, 127, 129, 130, 132, 133, 134, 135, 137, 138, 139, 140, 141, 142, 147, 154, 165, 180, 181, 186, 190, 198, 200, 201, 203, 206, 228, 229

gifted 104, 190, 192

Gift of Me 40, 42

giver 29, 52

giving 14, 17, 35, 42, 44, 50, 51, 52, 53, 58, 100, 115, 121, 131, 159, 168, 173, 180, 181, 186, 196, 199, 202, 203, 204

God xii, xiv, 5, 6, 7, 10, 15, 16, 17, 19, 21, 22, 25, 28, 29, 31, 32, 33, 34, 35, 45, 46, 47, 48, 49, 58, 60, 65, 67, 68, 69, 72, 73, 74, 75, 76, 77, 78, 79, 84, 85, 89, 92, 97, 98, 121, 124, 132, 137, 140, 145, 146, 147, 148, 165, 173, 174, 179, 181, 182, 195, 198, 214, 215, 221, 222, 223, 228

Godparent 61

goodwill 129

grace 11, 12, 76, 101, 203

grandfather 62, 135

grandmother 87

grandparents 103

grateful 4, 5, 22, 31, 33, 58, 100, 113, 164, 227, 228

gratitude 6, 7, 29, 30, 33, 34, 35, 39, 52, 60, 78, 102, 113, 115, 146, 147, 181, 198, 200, 206

greater good 64

greed 9

Greek God 194

grief xi, 68, 91, 97, 153, 179

grief process 153

ground 116, 117, 127, 156, 173, 191

grounding 116, 117

group setting 108, 109

growth xi, 3, 9, 23, 86, 94, 116, 156, 174, 178, 195, 202, 205, 228

grudge 23, 24, 103, 177

Guardian Angels 61, 62, 96

guidance xi, xii, xiv, 5, 7, 10, 17, 29, 30, 32, 46, 47, 48, 49, 60, 63, 65, 69, 74, 75, 79, 86, 103, 118, 127, 138, 141, 142, 145, 146, 147, 173, 194, 199, 227, 232

guide 3, 5, 7, 19, 22, 31, 47, 59, 60, 64, 78, 83, 109, 119, 127, 128, 130, 140, 141, 142, 145, 148, 158, 193, 196

guilt 15, 50, 52, 53, 97

gut feelings 32, 134, 139

H

habitat 190, 194, 195, 197, 199, 200

Hall of Records 60, 172

happiness xi, 4, 6, 7, 11, 13, 16, 18, 22, 26, 27, 29, 41, 58, 59, 68, 73, 94, 96, 97, 112, 166, 168, 174, 179, 191, 204

harmony 45, 48, 50, 84, 198

hatred 167, 170

Hawayo Takada 214

heal 17, 58, 74, 86, 87, 124, 174

healer 78

healing xi, xii, 13, 15, 16, 60, 70, 83, 84, 85, 86, 87, 95, 97, 102, 103, 108, 109, 113, 118, 124, 168, 177, 180, 199, 207, 209, 211, 213, 214, 215, 216, 218, 232

healing process 13, 16, 97, 109, 168, 211

Healing Spirit with Love 124, 180

health 11, 22, 78, 117, 174

healthy xi, 10, 11, 13, 17, 18, 26, 52, 54, 99, 164

hearing 17, 94, 105, 118, 122, 123, 127, 128, 133, 158

heart xi, xii, xiv, 5, 6, 7, 10, 14, 21, 30, 34, 35, 37, 40, 41, 44, 45, 46, 47, 48, 49, 52, 61, 66, 67, 68, 70, 79, 91, 92, 93, 96, 97, 102, 103, 115, 130, 142, 145, 152, 168, 175, 178, 179, 181, 183, 186, 190, 192, 197, 199, 201, 203, 207, 214, 227, 229

Heart Chakra 207

heartfelt 29, 31, 33, 75, 96, 146, 182, 183, 184

Heaven xii, xiii, xiv, 4, 6, 17, 20, 29, 58, 59, 61, 62, 63, 65, 66, 75, 76, 77, 79, 83, 84, 85, 86, 87, 88, 89, 90, 91, 92, 93, 94, 95, 96, 97, 98, 99, 100, 101, 102, 103, 104, 105, 106, 109, 112, 113, 115, 116, 118, 119, 122, 124, 132, 136, 140, 141, 153, 156, 157, 172, 173, 177, 180, 181, 192, 193, 197, 198, 204, 222, 223, 227, 229

Heavenly Support Team xiv, 7, 19, 25, 29, 30, 31, 32, 34, 35, 46, 47, 48, 49, 59, 63, 64, 65, 67, 68, 69, 70, 73, 75, 77, 78, 90, 139, 141, 144, 145, 146, 147, 148, 153, 155, 157, 159, 196, 211, 212

Heaven's Waiting Room 87, 88

Hell 84, 89

help iv, xii, 3, 4, 5, 6, 7, 8, 9, 10, 12, 13, 15, 16, 19, 21, 22, 25, 31, 41, 42, 43, 45, 46, 47, 51, 55, 56, 57, 58, 60, 61, 62, 63, 64, 65, 66, 67, 68, 69, 73, 76, 78, 85, 86, 87, 89, 90, 97, 100, 104, 106, 107, 110, 111, 113, 122, 124, 127, 130, 131, 137, 138, 140, 141, 142, 149, 153, 159, 168, 169, 170, 172, 173, 174, 177, 178, 179, 180, 181, 185, 186, 190, 194, 195, 204, 205, 207, 227

Hermes 195

higher purpose xi, 40, 42

honest 9, 10, 41, 42, 43, 44, 182, 227

honor 11, 44, 59, 113, 122, 123, 124, 178, 198, 217, 228

human journey xiii, 60, 67, 179, 182

I

idea xiv, 9, 11, 31, 32, 63, 73, 95, 96, 103, 126, 145, 147, 204, 205, 209, 211

identification 111

identify 100, 106, 108, 110, 130, 194, 195, 207, 208

identity 106, 107, 189, 231

illusion 159, 163, 165, 169, 177, 223

images iv, 32, 100, 106, 114, 118, 126, 127, 148, 153, 192, 206

independence 54, 55, 58

indicator 106, 107, 114, 119, 130, 191

in love 39, 43, 46, 48, 108, 128, 165, 168, 178, 223

inner peace 16, 45, 67, 75, 76

instant knowledge 114

instinct 9, 139, 231

intention 124, 146, 211, 212, 215, 218, 225

interact 191

interaction 179, 183, 184

internal 115, 149

interpret 101, 137, 150, 151, 155, 158

interpretation 137, 149, 151, 153

intuition xii, 10, 31, 32, 46, 47, 48, 49, 63, 79, 94, 121, 125, 127, 129, 130, 134, 139, 140, 141, 142, 145, 158, 190, 197, 231

intuitive 86, 95, 125, 141, 193

J

jealousy 9, 10, 166, 167, 189

Jesus 61

job 14, 15, 16, 30, 34, 54, 56, 57, 60, 62, 71, 84, 94, 95, 96, 99, 104, 106, 107, 128, 139, 179

John Holland 141, 228

journey xiii, xiv, 4, 5, 7, 24, 59, 60, 61, 66, 67, 83, 91, 96, 128, 130, 132, 142, 144, 155, 169, 172, 179, 182, 194, 203, 222, 227

joy xiv, 22, 29, 34, 35, 41, 44, 45, 58, 59, 62, 78, 86, 88, 96, 100, 144, 146, 152, 165, 179, 181, 189, 191, 204, 223

Jump-Start Your Intuition 141, 231

K

kindness 9, 10, 11, 12, 13, 40, 41, 54, 77, 170, 174, 179, 183

knowing xii, 3, 6, 15, 17, 35, 44, 59, 66, 67, 75, 89, 90, 91, 96, 97, 101, 106, 120, 121, 133, 134, 139, 179, 183

knowledge 43, 46, 62, 72, 77, 83, 88, 91, 93, 94, 103, 104, 109, 114, 119, 123, 124, 141, 172, 194, 198, 225

L

language 101, 131, 189, 190, 191, 192

Laura Day 141

lawyer 123

lesson 4, 9, 17, 21, 24, 26, 39, 54, 58, 60, 63, 65, 68, 77, 84, 86, 87, 94, 99, 137, 164, 167, 170, 171, 172, 173, 174, 186, 198, 202, 203, 204, 206, 227, 229

letters 56, 93

life path 32, 46, 69

life purpose xiv, 3, 50, 72, 91, 124, 138, 142, 163, 172, 181, 213, 222

Light v, xiv, 5, 8, 19, 25, 32, 35, 40, 42, 44, 45, 47, 49, 74, 76, 77, 83, 86, 87, 89, 97, 99, 105, 112, 113, 115, 118, 126, 132, 140, 146, 159, 178, 182, 183, 189, 201, 209, 212, 214, 215, 218, 222, 223, 225, 227, 228, 229

listen xii, 8, 10, 11, 31, 32, 46, 47, 49, 59, 63, 79, 106, 129, 141, 144, 145, 158, 159, 163, 173, 184, 185, 200, 202

listening 46, 75, 144, 157, 183, 185

live in the present 11, 20, 21

loss 15, 57, 67, 91, 92, 97

loss of a job 15

love v, xi, xii, xiii, xiv, 7, 13, 16, 17, 18, 29, 30, 32, 34, 35, 37, 39, 40, 43, 44, 45, 46, 47, 48, 51, 52, 53, 54, 55, 56, 58, 60, 62, 64, 65, 66, 67, 74, 75, 76, 77, 83, 90, 95, 96, 97, 100, 101, 102, 103, 104, 108, 109, 112, 113, 115, 118, 120, 121, 124, 128, 132, 134, 135, 138, 144, 145, 146, 147, 154, 159, 161, 163, 165, 166, 167, 168, 170, 171, 172, 173, 174, 175, 176, 177, 178, 179, 180, 181, 182, 189, 190, 193, 194, 195, 205, 206, 208, 211, 214, 221, 222, 223, 225, 227, 228, 229, 231

loved one xii, 7, 15, 47, 59, 62, 63, 74, 83, 84, 85, 86, 87, 91, 92, 93, 94, 95, 96, 97, 98, 100, 104, 105, 106, 107, 109, 110, 111, 112, 113, 119, 120, 121, 122, 123, 127, 132, 134, 140, 148, 153, 154, 158, 179

Love is in the Earth 208, 231

loving 7, 9, 17, 25, 31, 45, 54, 58, 63, 69, 74, 100, 103, 130, 146, 198, 228

lyric 128, 157, 158

M

manifestation 3, 6, 33

mannerism 131

martyr 166

mathematician 95

medical iv, 78, 123, 217

medicine 61, 217

Medicine Men and Women 61

meditating 144, 145, 199, 200

meditation 60, 63, 143, 144, 145, 147, 202, 203, 204

Medium xi, 16, 58, 70, 71, 72, 89, 94, 100, 102, 104, 105, 108, 110, 111, 112, 113, 114, 116, 118, 119, 120, 121, 122, 123, 124, 125, 130, 131, 137, 138, 180, 190, 225, 228

Mediumship xii, xiv, 62, 70, 72, 81, 86, 105, 110, 117, 120, 121, 122, 123, 124, 137, 138, 180, 192, 228

Melody 208, 231

memories 87, 107, 120, 125, 134, 148, 150, 158

memory 118

Mercury 195

messages xii, 10, 14, 49, 62, 63, 70, 71, 75, 89, 93, 94, 97, 100, 101, 102, 103, 105, 107, 108, 109, 110, 111, 113, 115, 117, 119, 120, 124, 125, 126, 127, 128, 130, 131, 134, 135, 137, 139, 140, 148, 155, 156, 157, 158, 159, 168, 192, 193, 194, 195, 196, 197

metaphysical 63, 85, 126, 146, 192

metaphysical gifts 63, 85

Michael 60, 232

Michele 85, 86, 119, 159

Mikao Usui 214

mind xi, 3, 4, 5, 6, 7, 9, 21, 22, 24, 25, 28, 30, 31, 32, 47, 48, 52, 65, 66, 72, 73, 74, 77, 93, 102, 103, 104, 105, 112, 115, 118, 120, 121, 126, 127, 128, 129, 133, 141, 142, 143, 144, 145, 148, 149, 150, 151, 152, 154, 155, 157, 158, 159, 168, 190, 203, 204, 211, 214, 215, 216, 217

mindset 176, 178

miracle 62, 140

mistake 11, 12, 24, 25, 39, 40, 43, 44, 168, 169

Mom-Mom 87, 134

money 30, 31, 34, 52, 53, 56, 57, 96, 144, 180, 181, 195

mother 35, 47, 58, 68, 116, 128, 129, 199, 200, 201, 202, 206, 227, 232

Mother Nature 35, 199, 200, 201, 206

Mother Theresa 68, 232

motivate 163

motivation 31, 51, 165

motivational factor 165, 170

mundane 140, 144, 145

murder 84

music 55, 127, 128, 130, 144, 156, 157, 159, 185, 200

musician 95, 157, 159, 217

N

National Geographic 189, 231

Nature iv, xii, xiv, 34, 35, 67, 122, 144, 150, 156, 158, 187, 191, 193, 197, 198, 199, 200, 201, 206, 207, 208

NDE 88

negative xi, 3, 4, 5, 6, 7, 8, 9, 12, 13, 16, 20, 21, 23, 25, 26, 27, 28, 31, 32, 40, 41, 42, 44, 47, 48, 68, 73, 75, 78, 79, 89, 128, 133, 140, 143, 150, 159, 164, 165, 166, 167, 168, 169, 173, 174, 176, 177, 178, 185, 196, 203, 204, 205, 209, 210, 211, 212, 229

negativity xi, 7, 9, 10, 23, 25, 26, 27, 28, 29, 41, 73, 94, 113, 133, 163, 166, 168, 183, 185, 215, 223

nightmare 150

not alone 15, 19, 59

nurse 78

O

object 127, 130, 149, 150, 151, 152, 167, 197, 205, 210, 211, 212, 221

obstacle 4, 6, 7, 16, 70, 76, 163, 166, 182, 204

ocean 34, 48, 50, 202, 203, 205, 206

open mind 7, 31, 65, 103, 104, 142, 148, 151, 152, 155, 204, 215

opportunities 3, 17, 20, 22, 29, 32, 33, 43, 64, 87, 139, 164, 166, 168, 195

opportunity xii, 12, 15, 22, 42, 76, 83, 84, 85, 86, 109, 113, 145, 153, 166, 171, 178, 206, 229

outlook xii, 3, 4, 30, 32, 78

outward signs 114

over-eating 13, 14, 15, 16

P

pain 9, 11, 12, 13, 14, 15, 16, 17, 23, 24, 25, 51, 55, 59, 64, 85, 87, 91, 93, 99, 102, 109, 130, 131, 164, 171, 173, 174, 215, 216, 222

paradise 84, 86, 99, 157

paranormal 112

parent 55, 56, 61

park 199, 200

passed away 112, 118, 159

Past Spiritual Masters 7, 59, 61, 83, 109, 140, 148

path 5, 10, 16, 17, 25, 27, 32, 46, 47, 48, 64, 69, 72, 128, 138, 142, 152, 163, 167, 196, 199, 203

patience 7, 16, 17, 54, 64, 65, 73, 79, 142, 190

patient 16, 67, 190

pattern 3, 7, 21, 40, 55, 173, 174, 176, 178

peace xi, 12, 16, 45, 66, 67, 73, 75, 76, 78, 84, 86, 87, 88, 92, 97, 103, 109, 112, 113, 143, 144, 145, 146, 176, 178, 200, 203, 212, 223

perfect 12, 16, 17, 52, 64, 65, 66, 69, 76, 130, 142, 153, 214, 216, 223

permission iv, 6, 29, 63, 108, 121, 122, 204

personality trait 106, 118

pessimism 5

pets 30, 34, 35, 99, 100, 126, 189, 190, 191, 195, 201, 203

phenomenon 87, 102, 110, 111, 140, 148

physical iv, xiii, 34, 73, 83, 84, 87, 91, 93, 97, 98, 99, 105, 106, 107, 109, 114, 116, 118, 119, 131, 134, 136, 164, 171, 174, 177, 189, 191, 195, 205, 209, 217

physical body 84, 87, 93, 109, 116, 217

physical characteristic 106, 195

plan xiv, 21, 32, 49, 60, 62, 64, 73, 79, 86, 104

poems 93

Pop-Pop 62

positive xi, 3, 4, 5, 6, 7, 9, 11, 12, 14, 16, 20, 21, 22, 23, 25, 26, 27, 28, 30, 31, 33, 39, 40, 41, 42, 48, 49, 51, 63, 69, 73, 78, 87, 103, 106, 123, 124, 150, 165, 166, 167, 170, 173, 176, 178, 179, 180, 184, 185, 196, 202, 203, 204, 211, 213, 215, 216, 229

positivity 28

potential 9, 20, 28, 58, 109, 171, 177, 178, 182, 196, 222, 223

poverty consciousness 30

power 4, 15, 18, 62, 76, 77, 167, 168, 202, 203, 206, 215, 221, 231

powerful 1, 3, 156, 165, 202, 205

Practical Intuition 141, 231

practice 5, 22, 35, 40, 41, 75, 79, 113, 119, 124, 137, 147, 148, 153, 154, 155, 158, 169, 180, 192, 203, 210, 211, 212, 215, 217

practitioner 78, 214, 215, 216, 217

prayer 16, 17, 21, 26, 29, 33, 59, 63, 64, 65, 66, 69, 74, 75, 76, 77, 93, 97, 139, 146, 167, 174, 177, 178, 179, 181, 223

praying 14, 60, 64, 65

prepare 71, 102, 110, 150

presence 4, 30, 34, 63, 67, 68, 69, 91, 100, 113, 118, 130, 131, 135, 140, 146, 191, 194, 196, 197, 198, 203, 228, 229

preserve 199

professional 15, 19, 52, 71, 78, 123, 137, 138, 169, 174, 208

psyche 26, 73, 190

Psychic 86, 110, 121, 137, 138, 190

psychic amnesia 110

purgatory 84, 89

Putting on Your Rain Slicker 133

R

rain slicker 133

Raphael 60, 232

rapid eye movement 148

reading xi, xii, 5, 58, 62, 71, 97, 100, 102, 103, 104, 106, 107, 108, 109, 110, 111, 112, 113, 114, 115, 116, 117, 118, 119, 120, 121, 122, 123, 130, 131, 225

reason 8, 10, 13, 14, 15, 30, 52, 56, 59, 83, 88, 104, 109, 117, 128, 149, 158, 163, 164, 165, 169, 171, 172, 181, 186, 209, 222, 225

receive xii, xiii, 11, 17, 31, 44, 48, 49, 51, 52, 53, 63, 65, 75, 76, 78, 87, 93, 101, 103, 108, 109, 113, 114, 120, 121, 125, 128, 134, 137, 139, 142, 146, 171, 181, 192, 204, 221, 229

receiving xiv, 17, 32, 45, 50, 52, 63, 71, 75, 85, 86, 100, 102, 103, 104, 107, 109, 110, 117, 118, 120, 122, 123, 125, 141, 146, 147, 158, 159, 197, 198, 215

recipient 103, 104, 111, 113, 114, 118, 119, 120, 131, 132, 180, 181, 192, 214, 215, 216

recognition 35, 86, 134, 164

recognize 4, 5, 12, 13, 15, 16, 17, 19, 22, 24, 27, 28, 30, 32, 33, 42, 45, 65, 68, 86, 88, 92, 95, 103, 106, 107, 125, 131, 134, 141, 143, 159, 164, 165, 166, 170, 171, 174, 198, 221, 228

reflection 153, 159, 167

regret 7, 20, 21

reiki 214, 215, 216, 217, 218, 225, 231

Reiki healing 216

Reiki Master 217, 225

rejuvenate 199

relating 182, 183

relationship 4, 10, 11, 12, 13, 14, 16, 25, 31, 34, 39, 45, 50, 51, 52, 53, 54, 55, 57, 58, 65, 69, 96, 100, 106, 111, 117, 123, 131, 147, 150, 167, 173, 174, 179, 189, 192, 195, 204

relax 42, 154, 206

religious 61, 76, 84, 89

reprogram 5

respect 11, 44, 51, 52, 54, 55, 58, 121, 122, 123, 124, 128, 164, 174, 178, 182, 183, 185, 198, 199, 200, 202, 215, 217, 227

respecting 12, 44, 46, 58, 200

responding 183

responsibility iv, 10, 12, 28, 54, 65, 166, 174

responsible 26, 27, 28, 168, 174, 213

reunion 58, 84, 85, 86, 94

reunite 65

review iv, xiii, 83, 85, 94, 222

Roman God 195

Root Chakra 214

S

Sacral 195, 214

Sacral Chakra 195

sadness 7, 64, 84, 89, 92, 101, 179, 189, 205

sage 210, 212

Saints 61

sanctuaries 199

sanctuary 199

scientist 95, 217

seeing 27, 34, 58, 60, 109, 126, 140, 141, 142, 144, 154, 197

self-esteem 10, 54, 58, 166

selfishness 8, 9

senses 48, 115, 117, 125, 126, 134, 157, 192, 202, 222

sensing of the truth 134

Sensitive 132, 190

serenity 17, 86

service 59, 71, 87, 123, 180

Shamans 61

sharing xiv, 30, 44, 47, 58, 60, 95, 107, 111, 117, 118, 120, 121, 122, 123, 157, 161, 165, 166, 172, 178, 183, 185, 228

shock 9, 92

sibling 58

sign 10, 14, 15, 22, 31, 32, 47, 48, 62, 63, 75, 79, 112, 114, 115, 126, 127, 134, 139, 141, 142, 159, 167, 193, 194, 195, 196, 197

significant other 34, 51, 171

signs 10, 22, 31, 32, 47, 48, 62, 63, 75, 79, 112, 114, 115, 126, 127, 134, 139, 141, 142, 159, 193, 194, 196, 197

sleep cycle 149

smell 48, 94, 114, 134, 136

smelling 134

smudging 210, 211, 212

solution xiv, 9, 11, 16, 24, 31, 32, 43, 95, 96, 145, 204, 205 soul xi, xii, xiv, 4, 8, 9, 12, 13, 14, 15, 16, 23, 24, 26, 28, 30, 33, 40, 45, 46, 47, 49, 50, 52, 60, 61, 64, 65, 66, 73, 74, 77, 83, 84, 85, 86, 87, 88, 89, 90, 94, 95, 96, 97, 99, 102, 119, 130, 139, 143, 144, 145, 156, 159, 163, 170, 171, 172, 173, 174, 176, 177, 178, 183, 186, 199, 201, 203, 204, 205, 213, 216, 221, 222, 223, 225, 227, 228

soul contract 9, 12, 87, 172, 176, 177

soul evolution 60, 61

soul evolvement 8, 77, 97, 163, 213

soul group 61, 84, 172, 176, 227

soul growth 86

soul lessons 65, 170

soul plan xiv, 60, 64, 73, 86

sound 34, 48, 57, 69, 76, 101, 106, 117, 118, 127, 128, 130, 156, 157, 177, 192, 200, 202, 206

Spirit v, xi, xii, xiii, xiv, 4, 7, 12, 15, 19, 23, 29, 32, 33, 34, 35, 40, 44, 45, 49, 50, 52, 53, 58, 59, 60, 62, 70, 71, 72, 75, 79, 83, 85, 86, 89, 90, 91, 93, 94, 95, 96, 97, 99, 100, 101, 102, 103, 104, 105, 106, 107, 108, 109, 110, 111, 112, 113, 114, 115, 116, 117, 118, 119, 120, 121, 122, 124, 125, 126, 127, 128, 129, 130, 131, 133, 134, 135, 136, 137, 139, 140, 143, 144, 145, 147, 148, 153, 154, 156, 157, 158, 159, 165, 167, 172, 176, 178, 180, 181, 182, 189, 190, 192, 193, 194, 197, 198, 199, 201, 202, 203, 205, 214, 216, 217, 218, 221, 222, 223, 225, 227, 228, 229

Spirit Guides 7, 59, 60, 83, 109, 119, 140, 148

spiritual iv, xiii, xiv, 7, 19, 54, 59, 60, 61, 62, 67, 76, 83, 85, 86, 87, 88, 91, 106, 109, 111, 115, 121, 122, 140, 144, 148, 169, 179, 189, 190, 193, 194, 197, 203, 207, 208, 209, 216

Spiritual Hospital 86, 87

spiritual journey 61, 91, 144, 169, 203

spouse 51

stage 3, 53, 70, 71, 92, 93

state of mind 9, 28, 30, 31

stream of consciousness 150

stress 14, 18, 117, 154

substitute for happiness 13, 18

suffering 18, 87, 93, 109

suicide 84, 85

symbol 63, 111, 118, 119, 120, 149, 150, 151, 152, 196

T

taste 15, 48, 94, 114, 118, 135, 136

tasting 135

Ted Andrews 194

telepathic 135, 136, 137, 190, 194

terminally ill 92

test 9, 67, 120, 208

theme 108, 152, 154, 197

the Source 9, 135, 143, 191

Third Eye 48, 126

thoughts xi, xii, xiv, 1, 3, 4, 5, 7, 9, 11, 13, 20, 21, 22, 23, 24, 31, 32, 41, 42, 44, 48, 54, 64, 65, 66, 73, 74, 75, 76, 78, 79, 92, 93, 95, 101, 106, 114, 118, 119, 121, 135, 143, 144, 145, 147, 148, 158, 185, 189, 192, 200, 203, 221

time xi, 6, 7, 8, 9, 10, 11, 12, 14, 16, 17, 18, 19, 20, 21, 22, 24, 26, 27, 28, 31, 32, 33, 34, 40, 41, 42, 43, 44, 45, 47, 51, 52, 53, 56, 57, 58, 59, 60, 63, 64, 65, 66, 67, 68, 70, 72, 73, 74, 75, 77, 79, 83, 84, 86, 87, 88, 90, 94, 95, 97, 98, 99, 100, 102, 103, 104, 105, 107, 109, 110, 111, 113, 118, 119, 120, 121, 122, 124, 126, 129, 130, 133, 135, 136, 138, 139, 141, 142, 143, 144,

145, 146, 148, 149, 151, 153, 154, 156, 157, 158, 159, 163, 164, 167, 169, 171, 173, 175, 177, 179, 180, 181, 183, 184, 185, 186, 191, 194, 195, 197, 199, 200, 203, 204, 205, 207, 208, 209, 216, 222, 223, 228, 232

touch 45, 93, 97, 116, 137, 156, 191, 214, 215

tough love 40, 55, 56

tragic event xi, 176, 177, 178

training 217, 231

transformation 97

transmit 107, 120, 131, 192

true love 39

true self 39, 48

trust 7, 8, 16, 17, 31, 33, 46, 53, 63, 65, 67, 68, 69, 72, 73, 75, 76, 79, 104, 120, 133

turmoil 9, 12, 76

U

under-eating 13, 14

United Nations 101

unity 176, 178

unwanted energies 203, 210, 211, 212

V

validation 106, 130, 134

veil 77, 83, 93, 103, 124, 140, 141, 168, 223

vessel 137, 180

vibration 116

vision 5, 6, 21, 32, 48, 101, 148, 216

visualize 6, 25, 41, 49, 74, 116, 126, 132

voice recorder 141, 150, 151

volunteer 53, 62, 84, 96, 99, 172, 180

W

well-being iv, 34, 54, 91, 180, 181

wisdom xii, 29

word association 151, 152, 154

worry 7, 20, 48, 49, 93, 107, 108, 111, 126, 149, 150, 152, 184

worthiness 204

worthy 17, 31, 45, 52, 75, 76

writer 95

www.HealingSpiritWithLove.com 124, 225

Y

Yahweh 221